AF515835

INDIAN FOREIGN TRADE

Trumped Up or Down

INDIAN FOREIGN TRADE

Trumped Up or Down

AMIYA CHANDRA

PENTAGON PRESS

Indian Foreign Trade: Trumped Up or Down
Amiya Chandra

ISBN 978-81-8274-906-1

First Published in 2017

Copyright © Amiya Chandra

All rights reserved. No part of this publication may be reproduced, stored in a retrieval system, or transmitted in any form or by any means, electronic, mechanical, photocopying, recording or otherwise, without the prior written permission of the Publisher.

Disclaimer: The views and opinions expressed in the book are the individual assertion of the Author. The Publisher does not take any responsibility for the same in any manner whatsoever. The same shall solely be the responsibility of the Author.

Published by
PENTAGON PRESS
206, Peacock Lane, Shahpur Jat
New Delhi-110049
Phones: 011-64706243, 26491568
Telefax: 011-26490600
email: rajan@pentagonpress.in
website: www.pentagonpress.in

Printed at Avantika Printers Private Limited.

"Om Namaha Shivaya..."

I offer to Shiva a respectful invocation of His Name

In his presence and with his blessings a journey started, may he be kind enough to show me the right path

May he keep me close to his heart and guide me with his divine light

May he destroy, that is so true to his nature, my pride and my fears

May he, as my father, protect me from the evil spirits of greed and pleasures

May he cleanse my soul, my mind, my heart and make me him—all eternal

I bow before you a thousand times, a million times as a beggar before the king

Shivaya, Shivaya, Shivaya

Om Namaha Shivaya

—Amiya Chandra

Contents

PREFACE

The 'America First Trade Policy'

The new Trump administration is still drafting a fresh Trade Policy for the United States of America and on March 2017, the office of the United States Trade Representative (USTR), released President Trump's Trade Policy agenda for 2017, which is as stated below:

> The office of the United States Trade Representative is committed to ensuring that American workers are given a fair shot at competing across the globe. USTR is working to reshape the landscape of trade policy to work for all Americans. On a level playing field, Americans can compete fairly and win. This new 'America First Trade Policy' will make it more desirable for companies to stay here, create jobs here, pay taxes here and rebuild our economy. Our workers and the communities that support them will thrive again, as companies compete to set-up manufacturing in the US, to hire our young people and give them hope and a real shot at prosperity again.[1]
>
> The 2017 Agenda outlines the new administration's four trade priorities: promoting US sovereignty, enforcing US trade laws, leveraging American economic strength to expand our goods and services exports, and protecting US intellectual property rights.[2]

The issued statement of the 2017 Agenda clearly demonstrates that the Trump administration is going to defend and promote American interests, and their appetite for globalisation is going to shrink further.

The bigger question is how it would impact world trade, and especially what it would mean for India... which is looking forward to expanding its exports to the United States, both for goods as well as services. The United States of America is the number one destination for exports from India, both in goods and services. Hence, any major policy shift towards restricting imports in the United States is going to adversely impact India.

It's critical for the Indian government, trade bodies, Indian industry and traders to get their act together in time to protect their interests and advance their objectives. India is positioned 18th in terms of American goods exports to India with a total share of less than 2 per cent of all American exports worldwide. The US goods trade deficit increased further by 4.2 per cent over the year 2015 and touched US$24.3 billion in 2016. The United States of America's thrust is to bridge this gap, which simply put, means that the US wishes to promote American exports to India and reduce imports from India; this is where the Indian interests start getting hurt.

Being the world's largest economy, America is, and will be important for expanding the Indian export base; the question is how?

The key to the Indo-US trade relationship hinges on Trump. The Indian Prime Minister is scheduled to meet the American President, and a lot is being anticipated from this meeting. The Indian Prime Minister had a very warm relationship with the previous US President; they both shared their vision through a joint statement in September 2014 to take the India-US bilateral trade relationship to US$500 billion a year by 2020. It was around US$109 billion in goods and services in 2015[3] and saw a decline in growth in the year 2016. The current level is just around 20 per cent of the target—much below the comfort level—and puts serious doubts on whether the target can be achieved at all.

India had great expectations and had started to warm up to the United States, despite the political resistance back home. India was willing to partner with the US to form a strategic economic relationship, which would have addressed all trade and security-related issues. However, the gap has been huge and despite the willingness demonstrated by both the State Heads, the actual progress has been too slow and too frustrating.

With Trump committing himself to a more protectionist, nationalistic, isolationistic approach, it is to be seen how the Indo-American relations grow, especially when many of Trump's commitments made during his election campaign go against India's interests. From that sense, it is important for the Indian government to understand and evaluate the changed scenario, re-align their objectives and approach. A warm relationship with Trump can help the Indo-US trade relationship transform itself to a new level altogether, and it can be an excellent opportunity for India. The question is at what cost and how, as Trump takes pride in being the best dealmaker and has made promises to the American citizens to protect American interests and to keep "America First".

This book tries to understand Trump as a dealmaker, and suggests how India can forge a new relationship with him and make deals that are mutually beneficial for both the nations. It also tries to identify opportunities as well as recommend a tentative approach that the Indian government can take.

END NOTES

1. Official website of USTR. https://ustr.gov/
2. https://ustr.gov/about-us/policy-offices/press-office/press-releases/2017/march/annualreport17
3. http://www.business-standard.com/article/news-ani/10th-india-united-states-trade-policy-forum-to-focus-on-bilateral-commercial-ties-116101800450_1.html

Acknowledgements

Humbly and with great respect and prayers, I thank my parents without whose blessings I never would have been able to achieve anything. It was my father's question on the eve of Trump winning the American Presidential election that triggered the idea for this effort. His question was simple:

"Is it Trump up or down for India?"

So the credit for this effort goes to my dear father.

I would also like to express my deepest gratitude to Pervinder Singh—without his continuous and dedicated support, this book would not have seen the light of day. Without his stewardship and persistence, I doubt this book could have been completed. He pushed and encouraged me whenever I would stop.

I will also like to thank my colleagues for their encouragement and the help extended to me.

I very respectfully acknowledge the efforts of other researchers, writers and journalists whose work I studied and have referenced. Any discrepancy or mistake on same account is unintentional, and I can only seek their forgiveness if that is the case. This book was written purely from an academic point of view, and any fault, omission, lapses or mistakes are all mine but unintentional and regrettable. The views expressed are mine and do not represent the views of the Indian government or any department of the government.

I am extremely grateful for my family for giving me all the support and love.

Lastly but most importantly, I would like to thank my publisher, Rajan Arya of Pentagon Press, for making this effort worthwhile and fruitful.

In the end, my sincere thanks to the readers and patrons of this book for showing faith in me.

AMIYA CHANDRA

INTRODUCTION

January 20, 2017, Donald Trump was sworn in by the American Supreme Court Chief Justice John Roberts as the 45th President of the United States of America, succeeding Barack Obama. The day was important not only for Americans, but for the world too. Donald Trump's victory was unpredicted; he was being considered an outsider the whole time while campaigning for the Presidential elections. He was running against Hillary Clinton, wife of ex-President Bill Clinton, and she herself had been Secretary of the State. She was fully supported and backed by Barack Obama whereas Trump was not even fairly backed by his own party during the campaign; the media had not been too kind to him either. Pre-election projections were predicting his defeat. It was a very bitterly contested election, which not only divided America on ideology, but made headlines across the world. He beat all odds and won the elections, and was finally sworn in as the President.

The bitterness in the election campaign was not only due to a clash of two personalities, but for reasons which had consequences for America, American allies and the world. Hillary Clinton, to a majority of people, meant the continuation of the eight-year-long Obama policies as Hillary had been an important part of the Obama administration, and had actively participated in formalising and promoting them. It would have meant no major surprises or shaking up of the world, the allies and friends of America, who could continue to pursue the policy decisions undertaken after long negotiations with the Obama administration. Whereas the campaign that Trump was running was anti-Obama policies, he promised while campaigning that he was going to repeal almost every major decision the

Obama administration had taken—be it healthcare, internal security, international security, immigration and most importantly, foreign trade deals.

Trump went hammer and tongs against Obama policies on foreign trade and squarely blamed them for all the ills that had overtaken America. He blamed job losses, closure of factories and huge economic losses to the American economy on Obama policies. He took a very aggressive stand by publically stating that he is going to repeal the North American Free Trade Agreement (NAFTA), Trans-Pacific Partnership Agreement (TPPA) and other multilateral treaties that the Obama administration had negotiated over the last few years. His campaign was seen and termed as negative, nationalistic, obstructionist and protectionist by the world community, especially from the foreign trade perspective. America being the number one world economy, any major disturbance there are bound to create ripples across the world, especially when the last decade has been economically and politically very turbulent and painful. The world was barely trying to come out of the Brexit shock, the Iranian nuclear deal and the trade recession, when suddenly Trump started a campaign which opposed globalisation, opposed free trade and focused on protecting American interest first. In his election campaigns, Trump was openly challenging the American allies, NATO and two close American friends—Japan and South Korea. He was threatening China with trade sanctions and a trade war; he was rooting for Brexit to the discomfort of EU; Mexico was rattled by his rhetoric against it and his promise to erect a wall for which he assured that the Americans would pay. All this was unnerving to the world.

India, too, has been watching with great interest, as in the last eight years of the Obama administration, there had been numerous initiatives undertaken by the Indian government. The current Prime Minister Mr. Narendra Modi shared a very healthy relationship with President Obama, and invested himself into this relationship to renew the Indo-US relationship. They both had agreed to work together and were committed to taking the bilateral trade to a new level. They announced in 2014 that India and the US are targeting a bilateral trade of US$500 billion per year. India and America had hardly started warming up to each other when

Trump was elected as the President of America, and finally sworn in as the President in January.

During his campaign, he had sent very mixed signals on India. At one point of time, he was full of praise for India, and vowed to work closely with Indians. At another point, he was blaming India for taking over the jobs of Americans through outsourcing. He blamed the Indian BPO industry for taking over the job of trained Americans at a fraction of the cost, which had forced the American companies to lay them off. He promised to raise the H1B visa fee and bring changes to discourage the outsourcing of jobs to India on H1B visas. He threatened to punish American companies with punitive actions and by levying heavy duties and taxes to discourage Indian companies.

His election is a big dilemma not only for India but for the world. India was committing itself to more globalisation, more openness in trade and was looking forward to expanding its trade relationship with the US. That, now, is a big question mark for India. What does the elevation of Trump as the President of United States mean for India? Is it good or bad news for India? How would his trade policies impact Indian exports to the US? What would be his stand on H1B visas and how would it affect the Indian service trade in the US?

It's been more than four months since Trump took charge; it has been a tumultuous ride so far for him, and the world is far more jittery and confused. The world leaders were hoping against hope that Trump would take a different approach once he is sworn in, and once he realises the responsibilities of his political position, the deeper nuances of the trade as well as political relationships. Trump, true to his poll promises, started rolling out presidential executive orders one after another. He retracted from the TPPA and gave instructions to review the NAFTA. He has been aggressive on the immigration agenda, and has been meeting business heads of American multinationals. He is using all the tricks to deal with them, cajoling and threatening them, luring them and dolling out the red carpet for a few of them. Till now, he has demonstrated that his adversaries have underestimated him; he is still maintaining the same stance that he had during the poll campaigning. He claims himself to be the biggest dealmaker and has promised American citizens to make great deals on behalf of them. That is, however, yet to be established.

He has also faltered on the way till now; his administration is being rocked by one controversy after another. His decisions have been challenged in many courts of America, and many of his orders have been either stayed or overturned. He has not backed down till now, and has been confrontationist in his approach and vowed to fight on. Despite being four months into his tenure, no one can yet predict his actions, nor is any one sure of the route he would take. This really is not what was expected.

I feel that there is a pattern to his approach; his approach is not going to be dictated by his subordinates or his administration, but by him. He loves to be in the driving seat and that is not going to change any time soon. Although by now the Indian government would have also activated its backroom channel diplomacy, I have a feeling that there is little clarity that it would have gotten by now. I feel it's important to decode Trump as a person before India engages with him directly. Thankfully, Trump is preoccupied with other domestic and international challenges at his hands, and India will be able to gauge his approach by then.

He has already met with the Canadian, the Japanese and the British Prime Minister, the German Chancellor, and shall be meeting the Chinese President very soon. He would have met other nation heads before he meets the Indian Prime Minister. This time in between is very important for India; not only will she have some time to fine-tune her approach but also have some time for back-room diplomacy to understand Trump's expectations and clearly put across her agenda to him. The most important meeting that India will have to wait upon is his appointment with the Chinese President. It would be interesting to know if he would still continue his diatribe against China for not being fair in foreign trade; will he chide it as he had promised during his poll campaign as a currency manipulator? Will he continue to threaten the Chinese with a trade war or is everything just going to fizzle out when reality dawns on him?

China has a very strong grip over American imports; over 22 per cent of American imports are from China. The Chinese President refused to take a call from the American President, unless Trump would commit to continue the 'One China Policy'. Trump, while being President-elect, had questioned the 'One China Policy' and even ruffled feathers when he took calls from the Taiwanese President to the great discomfort of China. However, it seems that the Chinese were able to reign him enough, as later when he was sworn in as the President, he backtracked and promised to continue with the 'One China Policy'; he also refused to call China a currency manipulator and, in fact, went ahead and asked for China's help against North Korea. All his aggressive posturing came to naught, and now things are more favourable for China politically, economically and in the international foreign trade relationship as well. Trump's moving out of the TPPA has been a boon in disguise for China, which is ready to occupy the space left vacant by Trump.

I feel that all these theatrics are a deliberate strategy of Trump; he believes in disruption, he is confident about himself and is not scared of mudding the water deliberately to measure the strength of his counterparts. President Trump claims himself to be the biggest dealmaker; he has promised the Americans a great number of deals that he is going to make. So how is that going to happen, and what do these deals mean for India?

Intent of the Book

There is too much of clamour surrounding Trump, created both by the media and his detractors. Despite his shortcomings, Trump has successfully managed to win the Presidential elections in America, and he must be credited for it. He has already clarified his intent to run for the second term as President, and as has been proven by history, the chances of him continuing are very high. This means that he would be at the helm of affairs for a possible eight years, and surely for the next four years.

It is in this context and view that India will have to deal with him and his administration. Thus, the intent of this book is as follows:

- Review Trump as a dealmaker and comprehend what it means for India. The section "Language of the Deal" covers this aspect.
- Propose an approach that India should take, based on our understanding. This has been covered in section "Patience is a Virtue".

- The "Need for Action" section in this book outlines few critical areas where India needs to have a holistic view for increasing its exports base. Although the subject is US-centric, many of the actions required to be undertaken by the Indian government are relevant for an overall exports growth in other parts of the world.
- "Move the Needle" section refers to the service sector's exports growth, as it has the potential to jump-start the Indian growth and help the Indian economy to leap forward.
- A brief summary and inferences are listed down in the final section titled "Conclusion", wherein an attempt has been made to provide a concise view on the way forward.

Outline of the Sections

The objective of this book is to understand Trump's approach to decision-making and dealmaking, and how India must look forward to engaging with him. In the section "Language of the Deal", we have tried to understand his approach to dealmaking, and we try to analyse his expectations while making a deal and how India should be preparing herself for Trump. *The Art of the Deal* has been a book co-authored by Trump, and he explains his own approach to making deals. Trump was already a successful realtor and businessman when he co-authored this book with Tony Schwartz in 1987. He rates this book quite high and close to him, and quotes quite extensively from it.

Although the Indian government wishes to deepen its trade ties with the United States, there are quite a number of challenges that both India and the United States of America continue to face. Every challenge is an opportunity in itself; the same is true in the Indo-US trade relationship. If strategically aligned, both India and the United States of America have tremendous growth opportunities. The objectives of the Indian Prime Minister could be equally matched and balanced by the objectives of the American President. Although in Trump, India has an opportunity to forge an excellent relationship and sign bilateral trade agreements with the US, the question is should India rush in or is it already late in its approach to Trump? In the section "Patience is a Virtue", we have tried to review an approach which may be suitable for India.

Wishing won't help India increasing its export base; concrete action is required on the ground. The approach till date has been piecemeal. It is quite unfortunate that till date, India is struggling with the basics and till date, no holistic approach has been framed and adopted. It has still not dawned on the policymakers that unless there is an integrated approach for the development of infrastructure to boost production and manufacturing, Indian exports cannot be increased to their real potential. Recommendations on key issues hindering the Indian trade growth have been listed in the section "Need for Action". Although the objective of this book has been to come out with some solutions to increase Indian exports in the United States, the reality is that issues highlighted in the "Need for Action" section are equally relevant for India's export to any nation.

Foreign trade in the services is on the rise all across the world, and India is a major stakeholder in this trade. It is amongst the top 10 exporters in the services sector, and its competitiveness and talent potential have the capability to push it into the top five. The services sector is increasingly becoming critical to the developmental trajectory of India. The World Bank has found that the sector's contribution in poverty alleviation is greater than that of agriculture and manufacturing. The service sector has an advantage over the manufacturing sector in terms of speed, lower capital investments and being technology-driven. The disadvantages are equally critical; it is more innovation-dependent. And, changes occur at a fast pace, i.e. its fall is equally quick, it is knowledge-driven and dependent upon talent and their iteration rates are high. The United States is the biggest importer of Indian services, especially for backend Business Process and Operation (BPO) services. The concerns over H1B visas is most crucial for the Indian IT sector that provides services in the US through placing its personnel in the US for onsite operations; any increase in fees or any restrictions imposed is going to hit them hard. There is a perception in the US that these Indian IT companies are like sweat shops, and that they are taking away jobs of the Americans as the American companies are outsourcing these jobs to the Indians at much lower costs and salaries.

The potential and scope to expand the services exports is tremendous in both, India and the US. This sector is much beyond the commonly mistaken BPO services. The section"Move the Needle" points to the key challenges that the Indian service exporters face, and how these challenges could be addressed. The section also tries to put forward suggestions on how India and the US companies can collaborate and benefit.

A brief synopsis of each of the sections is listed in the end section titled "Conclusion",wherean attempt has been made to put key points in a precise manner as a review of each section.

Scope of the Book

The scope of the book is limited to reviewing the current event of things postswearing-in of Trump as the US President, and its impact on the Indian exports to the US.

The book is general in nature and tries to assess the situation from a conceptual point, and not from a statistical point. There were three key reasons for the same:

- Firstly, the data is not consistent, and does not match when cross-referenced.
- Secondly, the idea was to highlight a more macro-conceptual approach; hence too much dependency on data has been avoided.
- Thirdly, I wished to keep the book simple, interesting and concise so that a wider reader base can be reached.

My intent has been to stir the thought process and contribute with whatever little understanding (or lack thereof) that I have of the current situation. There is a possibility of a few of these recommendations sounding old or repetitive... however, I have tried to put across a new angle and a new approach to them. Even if few of these recommendations are in the knowledge of the government and other stakeholders, the effort has been to re-stress on the urgent action required on them, without which there is little chance of witnessing India's export growth.

The book is my tribute to the people working tirelessly towards improving the Indo-US trade relations, and to those who are assigned the responsibility of taking this forward. My focus in this book has been on exports and Indo-US trade, and any recommendation is from that perspective. I understand that a relationship between two nations cannot solely be based on their trade potential, and that trade is dependent on many other factors, which are beyond the scope of this book.

The book is purely for academic pursuit, and a personal attempt to share and contribute personal insights. It has no relationship with the professional or official positions held. The suggestions, comments and recommendations are personal, and do not reflect the official stand of the Government of India or any of its departments.

Apart from personal experience and understanding, I have studied the research and study material available on online digital platforms as well as in print form through books and journals. I have tried to list references wherever I have referred to the works of others. The same has been done purely to substantiate my point of view. If any reference is omitted or there is a discrepancy, it is purely unintentional and I regret it.

The critique is also based on personal assessments and understanding from a positive viewpoint to understand the gap; any discrepancy from my end on this is regrettable and unintentional. The sole purpose of this book is to initiate a dialogue, discuss and debate on suggesting and finding new directions for bilateral trade development, and creating a strong foundation for economic and commercial engagement between the two democracies – India and the United States of America.

SECTION ONE

LANGUAGE OF THE DEAL

"I like thinking big. I always have. To me it's very simple: if you're going to be thinking anyway, you might as well think big" Most people think small, because most people are afraid of success, afraid of making decisions, afraid of winning..." —**Donald Trump**[1]

A deal in its traditional dictionary sense means an agreement entered into by two or more parties for their mutual benefit, especially in a business or political context.

The catch phrase here is "mutual benefit"; how can a deal be concluded when one of the parties entering the deal is not concerned with the mutual benefit of the deal, but only interested in safeguarding its own interest? Can such a deal be brokered, and is it possible for the other party to still get around the deal and ensure that mutual benefit is maintained and both the parties gain? As per my viewpoint, such a deal is possible, as I believe that it is possible to express and share contrary viewpoints and yet maintain a balance while dealing. The language and mode of engagement while dealing are the most critical aspects, and if enough flexibility is maintained, even tough deals can be concluded to the satisfaction of both parties.

The devil lies in detailing—getting into any deal without evaluating the other party and not being adequately prepared can be dangerous, especially when dealing and settling terms of international trade.

Thankfully, here the leader of the other party—President Trump of the United States of America—takes pride in being a "Deals man". He claims for aiming high and thinking big. He has himself claimed that he understands making deals more than anyone else, and that his administration is going to forge new deals that would be of great benefit to America and would protect the American interest. He has put across his thoughts in a book titled The Art of the Deal, and has explained at length his approach to making a deal. Although the book is about Donald J. Trump in the capacity of a person, realtor and a businessman, dealing with other nations of the world as the President of the United States is a different matter altogether. Yet it does shed light on the approach of the person the Indian government will have to deal with, and provides insight into his behavioural characteristics.

Following are few pointers from his book, on how he perceives himself and how the Indian government can thus prepare itself:

1. Flexible in Approach

> *"I also protect myself by being flexible. I never get too attached to one deal or one approach. For starters, I keep a lot of balls in the air because most deals fall out, no matter how promising they seem at first. In addition, once I've made a deal, I always come up with at least half a dozen approaches to making it work because anything can happen, even to the best-laid plans."*[2]

From this excerpt, it shows that Trump has an open-ended approach like any person who wishes to close deals on his terms.Yet he knows that there would be many compromises that he or the other party may have to make. He won't rush into even a best-laid deal and evaluate it from his angle and if it suits him, he will close it soon. This should be heartening to India, especially to the Prime Minister of India who hails from Gujarat, where the art of dealmaking is in the genes. Keeping an open approach is suitable to India too, as it opens a window to view things in perspective and from multiple angles. It is simple: while dealing with President Trump or his administration, all things will have to be kept simple, precise and short. The Indian government will have to do its homework and must have multiple approaches or solutions well thought of from the beginning.

The approach of the Indian PM and the Indian government would have to be personal, positive and pre-planned.

2. Know your Market

> *"I like to think I have that instinct. That's why I don't hire a lot of number-crunchers, and I don't trust fancy marketing surveys. I do my own surveys and draw my own conclusions. I'm a great believer in asking everyone for an opinion before I make a decision. I ask and I ask and I ask, until I begin to get a gut feeling about something. And that's when I make a decision."*[3]

We can construe from this that Trump is not a follower of tradition; he has a mind of his own and though he may consult the American experts on India on trade issues with India, he is going to be deciding from his own experience. He is not going to conduct business the way the previous American governments have. This can be an advantage for India if the Indian PM is able to convince him about the American Indian Strategic Trade Partnership, and if he has a really worthwhile deal to offer to him. For India, this means that the government must focus on the people who surround Trump, and must create a positive influence about India. The Indian mission in the US must not miss even a single opportunity to connect with Trump or his administration. Small capsules on how India and American trade can be taken forward must be created and shared.

It also means that whenever the chances occur, the Indian PM must engage directly with Trump, and put across carefully the progress India has made,how the two nations can mutually benefit each other and how the objectives of Trump can be easily achieved and balanced. This would have to be done in the most personal of ways, as it is widely known that Trump has very strong likes and dislikes. He likes to know the person whom he is dealing with, and if the thought process matches, the chances of making the deal are much more. There is much to learn from how the Canadian, the Japanese and the British Prime Minister met with him and generated a warm relationship. This,especially when Trump has called off the TPPA (which had a negative impact on Japan); when the NAFTA is being relooked at (the Canadian interests appear at risk) and Brexit had put Britain at differences with the EU and it needed the American support for trade.

The Canadian PM was well aware of Trump's stance towards NAFTA; he did a smart thing by avoiding a confrontation or direct discussion on it, and ideated on Women's Empowerment in Canadian-American Trade relationship through a "Women's Entrepreneurship Initiative". A very intelligent strategy adopted by him was to find a common ground where both the parties could agree upon and drive mileage; where both would benefit too.

India, too, must try to find common ground wherein a positive start can be made between the two heads of the nation; "Collaboration, not Confrontation" should be the mantra when dealing with Trump. India must assess and try to understand Trump's expectations from it, and it would do India no harm if some of those expectations can be fulfilled within the first meeting of the American President and the Indian Prime Minister.

The Trump administration is equally aware that India is keen that Trump waters down the impending restrictions on the H1B visas, which he has publically stated to tighten and further his poll promise of "Hire American". This hardening of stance is not new to India, and successive American presidents before Trump had also tried to add restrictions. In the existing US Congress, there are bills already introduced that aim at restricting the H1B visas and have political support from both, the Republicans and the Democrats. These bills are designed to discourage US companies from hiring skilled immigrants at a lower salary than their American counterparts, and to deny American workers jobs in America.

So the writing has been on the wall for a while for India's IT industry, which is too dependent on the H1B visas; they should have and would have planned strategies to deal with such an eventuality by now. The Indian PM should be careful and not make the H1B issue a major point of confrontation with the new administration as there are many other green shoots visible which India should nurture.

Since India's bilateral trade with the US is approximately around a sixth of China's trade with America and less than 2 per cent of what America trades worldwide, unless Trumps sees a substantial advantage in India, he is unlikely to take trade with India seriously. This is precisely why the initiative would need to be taken by India to a bilateral trade agreement, sans the H1B visa relaxations. Simple common sense points that sooner or later, the Trump administration would realise the futility of such protectionist measures as they would lead to either rising costs for the American companies and turning them expensive and uncompetitive, or many of such jobs will move to robots or systems with Artificial Intelligence... hence, not resulting in any increase in jobs. There's a high chance that American business houses themselves may lobby for India as they understand the repercussions of these measures.

As Lisa Curtis, Senior Research fellow at the Asian Studies Center of the Heritage Foundation, puts it: "Hopefully, the two sides can find a way forward to both, protect American workers and also continue a programme that is important for the US economy and a major building block for relations between the two countries."

3. Protect the Downside; The Upside will Take Care of Itself

> *"People think I'm a gambler. I've never gambled in my life. To me, a gambler is someone who plays slot machines. I prefer to own slot machines. It's a very good business being the house.*
>
> *It's been said that I believe in the power of positive thinking. In fact, I believe in the power of negative thinking. I happen to be very conservative in business. I always go into the deal anticipating the worst. If you plan for the worst—if you can live with the worst—the good will always take care of itself."*[4]

Although the actions or comments by Trump and his administration may seem too erratic or spontaneous to the common man, there is a sure-shot deliberate calculative stance in it. Very cleverly, they are building out and checking out the minimum acceptance levels within the various stake-holders, gauging their response and then after assessment, they would make a move. They surely are throwing lots of balls in the air—nobody knows how many they will catch, but if carefully observed, they seem to throw many balls in the air, prepared to live with it as they are sure to catch one back, and if any other lands into their lap, then their objective is achieved.

India is barely around 2 per cent of value of foreign trade that America trades worldwide; and there too, is a trade deficit for the Americans. So expecting too many concessions from the Trump administration is really foolhardy, unless the Indian government comes with a strategic plan that catches Trump's imagination. America is India's number one trade partner, so the onus lies on India to take the relationship to the next level. India here cannot afford to follow the conventional style of diplomacy and approach with Trump, and must work on four key pivots:

Get personal: Modi must forge a personal relationship with Trump, and this thankfully should not be too difficult as both he and Trump have many similarities; both are viewed as outsiders in the political circles, unconventional, both are nationalists, key decision-makers without any real political or leadership challenge, have a good backing from industrialists and business houses, workaholics, and easily accessible. The time is also opportune as both have time to see through the implementation of their agendas.

Aligned administration: The most frustrating thing for any leadership is to see its good work being undone by a non-aligned bureaucratic set-up. It will be easier to achieve Indian goals if an empowered group of trade negotiators is set-up with a singular focus to take forward the agenda set by the Indian Prime Minister and the US President. The group shall be given a clear brief, and the rest shall be left to it to detail out in strictly outlined timelines.

Proactively set-up the agenda: The Indian government should multiply its efforts, and must proactively set the agenda and should be guided by the "Collaboration, not Confrontation" mantra. Both India and the US have genuine issues: both have put across trade barriers, and the agenda should be not to catch the bull by the horns but to let it run free in an open field, and harness its energy and strength to break new ground, to seed new opportunities. The Indian government is, and shall continue to utilise multiple channels to understand the expectations President Trump has from India.

Solution mode: The Indian government will have to do prior groundwork on issues thatare key for American administration, and will have to chart out multiple solution approaches beforehand. For example, if Trump asks to open up the Indian market to American businesses, then which are the key sectors that the Indian government would be willing to open?And in return, what would be India's expectation? Any or all the solutions must align with Trump's objectives as well as safeguarding Indian interests. Being overprotective or too guarded is not going to serve India's purpose.

4. Maximise Options

"Aim for the moon, and you can at least be sure of collecting coconuts in your bags" is a very popular saying in India, and the same is true for Trump. By aiming high and being flexible, he has maximised options for himself. He is a smart businessman and realtor, and knows that unless one setshis/her targets many times over the expected results, they will never be sure of achieving the target. He is mentally prepared for many of the deals to fall through; he just ensures that there are multiple approaches to securing the deal so that chances of making a deal increase without compromising on the target. As a realtor, he had prepared multiple plans for his estates and if one approach failed, he was quick to adapt and suggest the next – till the time he got what he always wanted as the end-result. He had neither stuck to one approach nor to an idea– he had simply prepared beforehand, and offered multiple solutions to the same estate. And in the end, was mostly successful in getting the best out of the estate, making profitable deals.

The Indian government must understand that in Trump, there is a unique opportunity for India as well as America to undertake an unconventional and radical approach to mutually benefit and increase their trade base. The Indian government should prepare multiple trade blueprints, each with a different design and approach to the issues that are holding back the Indo-American trade relationship. We can be sure that under Trump, the American administration would also be keen to take a similar approach.

For example, in pharmaceuticals, both India and USA have divergent contrary views. While the American administration wishes for a strict Intellectual Property Rights (IPR) implementation to protect its interests, the Indian administration has a different challenge and priority on their hands. India is a signatory to Trade-Related Aspects of Intellectual Property Rights (TRIP), and to move beyond this commitment currently is not in its interest. So there is currently a dead-end, and both the nations are rigid on their stand. This needs to be resolved and both nations have to rework their strategies and approaches to this issue.

India itself is a developing country, with a huge population which needs new treatments, new medicines, etc. at a much cheaper cost than what the American companies offer. This is also true for every developingnation in the world. The Indian pharmaceutical companies have been able to develop generic medicines at a fraction of the costs to the Americans, and are now exporting them worldwide, and therein lies the conflict of interest. Although India is signatory to TRIPS and in compliance with the World Trade Organisation (WTO) agreement, the American companies push the American administration to leverage their financial interests and want a tighter IPR regime. This is hardly going to succeed as the Indian government is well aware of the necessity to keep drug prices under control for itself and other developing nations' patients.

The cost of American medicines is not so much about the raw material or technology as much as being influenced by royalties or heavy costs that they charge on R&D. The Americans justify this as their rightful rewards on innovations, research and development. It's true that the R&D in medicine is a long, hard task, and getting it approved from various medical and trade bodies takes too much time and heavy investments. But sadly, it is also true that the American companies charge a hefty fee, and that puts the medicine out of reach for a majority of patients who may need the cure, especially in poor and developing economies of the world. For example, the patented triple-combination therapy medicines for HIV/AIDS cost US$10,000 per person per year in industrialised countries, while generics can be purchased across the developing world for less than US$200 a year.[5]

The most-quoted argument put across by the American pharmaceutical companies is that of heavy investments put into their R&D.

> *"Only one out of 10,000 experimental compounds in development will reach the marketplace – at a cost, according to one recent analysis, of $1bn (£642m) for each medicine approved. Thus, each successful molecule that makes it as a drug needs to pay for the thousands of molecules that fail ... Without patents, investment in R&D will plummet and people suffering from diseases without effective options will be left without hope. Simply put: without patents, there will be no new medicines for untreated diseases and no new generics."*[6]

This prompts the local pharmaceutical companies in the developing nations to produce generics or tweak the formula just a bit to escape the IPR. The Indian government in the interest of its citizens' health provides access to cheap medicines for the majority of its poor population, and promotes and encourages these local pharmaceutical companies to develop and manufacture them.

American companies have this impression that the Indian pharmaceutical companies will flood the domestic and international markets with cheaper generics in absence of weak IPR laws in India, and are wary of setting up exports and manufacturing bases here. The reality lies mid-way. The American companies are also guilty of ever-greening of their patents by adopting dubious strategies, and these companies introduce cosmetic changes and are able to retain their patents, denying millions of patients access to cheaper medicines and cure. Such companies are driven purely by greed and profit without any social accountability. Countries like India stand against such malpractices, whereas the American administration continues to support such companies, and hence, the conflict never gets conclusively resolved.

This gridlock can be brought down together by the American President and the Indian Prime Minister through the introduction of a tiered pricing framework for manufacturing and exports within India and worldwide. A tiered-pricing formula can provide a "win–win" solution to both the nations, protect their national interests and push for new innovations and R&D, yet maintaining affordable access to medicines. The pharmaceutical companies in both nations will also gain from such an initiative, as the tiered-pricing framework will enable a transparent and coherent interpretation of the law.

A joint mechanism– with stakeholders from the industry, healthcare, patient rights protection groups, legal experts, trade experts, etc. under the umbrella and guidance from the Indian and American administrations– can help formalise the tiered-pricing system. Fair pricing, promoting competitiveness, safeguarding intellectual property and promoting innovation should be the objective and must be evaluated on socio-health and socio-economic considerations. Tiered-pricing should be so targeted that manipulations and fraud in pricing are minimised, and heavy penalties are imposed to deter any wrongdoing.

The Indian pharmaceutical companies still lack an R&D infrastructure, labs and trial mechanisms, which have moved on and seen tremendous sophistication and data analytics in developed countries. The Indian companies are still way behind on the innovation curve for new medicines, machines and technology. These are the areas where the American pharmaceutical companies excel and can be of great help to India. For future growth of the Indian Pharma, we need these American companies to set their base in India, support R&D here and help the Indian industry grow further.

The American and Indian administrations must set up a conducive environment through a clear policy framework, so that the pharmaceutical industry can work together and benefit from each other's expertise. The two governments must become facilitators for new joint ventures to set up and boost jobs, research and production efficiency. The scope and potential are tremendous on both ends. The bilateral agreements between India and America in pharmaceuticals and healthcare itself can be a big game changer.

5. Use Your Leverage

> *"The worst thing you can possibly do in a deal is seem desperate to make it. That makes the other guy smell blood, and then you're dead. The best thing you can do is deal from strength, and leverage is the biggest strength you can have. Leverage is having something the other*

guy wants. Or better yet, needs. Or best of all, simply can't do without. Unfortunately, that isn't always the case, which is why leverage often requires imagination, and salesmanship. In other words, you have to convince the other guy it's in his interest to make the deal."[7]

Every seasoned salesman in the world would agree with Trump here. No doubt about it! It is especially so if the salesman wishes to benefit out of the deal. To use leverage, a person requires some understanding of a product or service, understanding of psychology, human behaviour and his target customer, and most of all, be prepared.

It is common saying in marketing that you get exactly seven seconds to catch attention. Those first seven seconds are important, and if you don't catch the eye (attention) of your potential customer, the chances of success are dismal. All the successful companies understand this, and for the same reason go to extreme research and analysis to understand the aspects they can leverage for their products or services, against the competition. They develop strategies around these leverages and market them; they develop marketing plans around them and evaluate them; they continue to find new leverages as the consumer preferences change. If they are not alive to it, they disappear.

What is true for them is true for exports too. If the Indian government or Indian exporters are keen to increase their export base, they will have to identify their leverage. They will have to identify what it is that they have that the buyer wants. It is not the product or the service, it's the leverage. Many of the great products and services have failed in the market because they couldn't establish leverage for their products or services against their competition.

Trade in simplest term is an exchange and fulfilment of the trading parties' needs and requirements. One can only trade if one has something that the other party needs and similarly, the other party has something that we need. This basic concept is the starting point of leverage.

What is it that India has that America needs, and what does America have that we need?

Trump has been very vocal about protecting American interests, promising job protection to Americans and an increase in American manufacturing and exports. This is not unusual, as the same is what the Indian government is vocal about – protecting Indian interests, promising job growth and increasing Indian manufacturing and exports. These expectations are not exclusive to India, America, China or others, but for every single government. At the end, it all boils down to the ground reality of "need vs. fulfilment" or "availability gap vs. available capacity".

The biggest leverage that India has is "a market" to trigger further American growth. India has huge gaps in its urban infrastructure, defence, energy and power, healthcare and pharmaceuticals, telecommunications, sports infrastructure, etc., which can be catalytic in the American exports growth to India, and at same time fulfil India's requirements. Similarly, the American market is equally attractive for India, i.e. for its services, IT, handicrafts, processed foods, textiles/apparels etc. Looking minutely into the requirements and available capacities for both the nations, it can be put across as following:

a) India has potential and requirements at the upper end of the value chain for services and products, which the Americans can fulfil and through it, can balance their trade deficit.
b) India is strong in fulfilling the lower and mid-end of value chain for services and products, through which it can help America be more competitive and capture more market share in other developing and emerging economies of the world. India can help America balance its over-dependence on China, Mexico and Canada, which together control the majority of American imports, and with whom America has huge imbalance and trade deficits.

If both the nations are going to be protectionist and create hindrance or trade barriers for each other, theyare going to falter and lose an excellent opportunity that time has presented them with. Both will have to be magnanimous and farsighted in their approach. If India seeks the H1B visa access to the American market for its services, it will simultaneously have to be open about providing similar access to the Americans, enabling them to offer their services in India, for example in architecture, legal services, healthcare, engineering etc. Similarly, if America seeks India to open up its market for American goods, then it will have to be open to the

Indian goods too. There is a possibility that some of the business sectors in both the nations may have to be realigned and become more competitive in their domestic markets to remain relevant, but then the opportunity is too big for both the nations to be myopic towards the larger goal.

India is dependent on imports for its defence requirement, and is currently the largest importer of defence equipment. At one point of time, Russia was the biggest defence supplier to India, even though India's basket was open to many other countries like France, United Kingdom, Israel, Italy, etc. Recently, the United States has edged out Russia as India's largest defence supplier, and the possibility of taking this relationship to the next level is very high.

Both India and America have strategic interest in maintaining balance in the world, particularly in Asia. China has not been shy of baring its ambitions and domination in Asia. China's defence spending has grown; it has taken an aggressive stand on numerous issues and has tried to cow down others with its defence powers. It has undertaken an extensive modernisation of its defence system and the expansion of its arsenal—this may not be an immediate threat to India and the United States of America but China, for sure, is trying to tilt the balance in its favour and has ambitions to be another superpower and stand up to the US. The Trump administration and Indian government are both aware of it in one way or the other.

Putting defence purchases from the United States on the table can be helpful in grabbing Trump's attention; this will serve his goals as well. All three wings of the defence forces have huge requirements, and the Indian government can extend a government-to-government deal to Trump. The purchase of new American fighter jets should be on the cards, and will reassure the American President that India can help him create more jobs for Americans for short as well as the long term. Submarines, ships, helicopters, drones, artillery, small and heavy arms etc.—the list is long and the opportunity to grab business, tremendous.

The aviation sector in India is growing at a very fast pace. India's domestic air passenger traffic was at 100 million in 2016, overtaking that of Japan (97 million), and was behind only to the US (719 million) and China (436 million).[8] It's the world's third largest aviation market; this is when India has barely woken up. With economic growth and increase in India's middle class population, the aviation sector has the potential to grow many times over. The demand for aeroplanes, airport infrastructure, etc. is going to jump manifold. This again is an excellent opportunity for America.

The Indian aviation sector's growth is promising for the US companies across the aviation sector—manufacturing (planes, component manufacturers, technology, equipment etc.) and the American maintenance, repairs and operations value chain. The American companies will benefit by setting up their base in India or sourcing from Indian companies and setting up engineering centres in India to tap into the large and relatively cost-effective talent pool available in India.

For example, according to Boeing, the demand for new aircraft in India is expected to be 1,850 planes valued at US$265 billion over the next 20 years, of which 84 per cent would be single-aisle narrow body aircrafts. This translates to USD 240 billion of aircraft orders over the next 20 years. Boeing's market share in India is above 40 per cent, and it dominates the wide-body segment. It sources more than half a billion dollars' worth of components and services from 30 direct and over 100 indirect suppliers in India. The value of sourcing is expected to double by 2020.[9]

Robotics, energy and environment, advance engineering, transportation and logistics, healthcare etc. are few other sectors where India is seeking help and investments. These are not only high potential investment sectors but also where the American exports can benefit.

The Indian government simultaneously must push the Americans to open up to Indian products and services, especially those sectors which are heavily dependent on physical labour—like agriculture, food processing, textiles, apparels, leather and footwear, handicrafts, handloom, etc. The barriers that have been put across by the American administration should be lowered in selective sectors. In fact, the American exporters and manufacturers can collaborate and form joint ventures with Indian counterparts for the products on the high end of the value chain for India.

Like engineered textiles, geo-textiles etc., they will gain from the frugal engineering that Indians excel in.

6. Enhance Your Location

> *"Perhaps the most misunderstood concept in all of real estate is that the key to success is location, location, location. Usually, that's said by people who don't know what they're talking about. First of all, you don't necessarily need the best location. What you need is the best deal. Just as you can create leverage, you can enhance a location, through promotion and through psychology."*[10]

Geographically, it is not possible to shift a location, except that a good purpose for a location can be identified and taken advantage of.

The market size and its location matters in international trade. Mexico and Canada share boundaries with the United States, and hence, have a geographical location advantage as it helps in bringing down the time, transportation and logistics costs, both for material and labour. China, too, has a shorter access route to the United States than India. Hence, there is a natural advantage available to the three big competitors for India for the American trade share. The same is true for the American exporters as China shares a boundary with India and has much better access to the Indian sea ports.

China is at an advantage, than is America or India. Add to it the easy Chinese visa access for traders and businessmen in China. This is one of the key reasons as to why China has been able to push exports to both India and America, whereas because of its policies and a lack of infrastructure, India has not been able to push its exports into China as well as the USA.

Comprehensively, both America and India would need to look into their policies to improve trade access via making travel easy, and by improving their logistics and transport mechanism. China had made an effort to set up a complete infrastructure to boost its export to all parts of the world. It has successfully been able to set up a dedicated rail and sea corridor for having access to its European, Middle-Eastern and African markets. It is pushing aggressively for creating new maritime routes and ports for its exports, as well as for sourcing cheap raw material from Africa and other Asian countries. China has been more successful in forming trade and political alliances which benefit its business whereas both, the American and Indian administration, has a lot of catching up to do with China's approach.

America and India can benefit mutually if they are able to form a reasonable trade alliance, wherein American companies can increase their export penetration in Africa and Asia by setting up base in India. Not only the exports, but the American companies would also be able to import easily from India, as they would have the price advantage of lower input costs. The Indian manufacturers, importers and exporters, too, would benefit by not only increasing the Indo-American trade, but by partnering with the American companies for expansion of their exports footprint in Africa and other Asian countries.

The southern peninsula of India protrudes into the Indian Ocean, which helps India to establish close contact with West Asia, Africa and Europe from the western coast and with South-East and East-Asia from the eastern coast. The only negative factor is India sharing its boundary with a very hostile nation—Pakistan, which is a close ally of China and has even permitted China to build ports and a road network through its territory. Unfortunately, the history of America supporting Pakistan against India is quite fresh in the minds of Indians and as a result, there is lack of faith in Indians over American intentions.

India being a large country has geographical, climatic and socio-economic diversity, and a long coastline as well, which are perfect for creating new infrastructure to support the Indo-American businesses. It has five major seasons and many micro-climatic geographical locations, where a variety of products can be produced. It is rich in many natural minerals and ores. Having a considerable English-speaking population, and with laws written in English language, makes it easier for American companies to communicate and trade. Its strong workforce of engineers and software professionals has helped India become the power-center in the IT services trade. Indians are slowly but steadily moving up the value chain in IT and communication engineering and software development.

This will again be beneficial for American companies by bringing in talent at a better cost and increase their efficiency and productivity, hence making them more competitive. America has as much to gain as it will benefit the Indian trade.

7. Get the Word Out

> *"You can have the most wonderful product in the world, but if people don't know about it, it's not going to be worth much. There are singers in the world with voices as good as Frank Sinatra's, but they're singing in their garages because no one has ever heard of them. You need to generate interest, and you need to create excitement. One way is to hire public relations people and pay them a lot of money to sell whatever you've got. But to me, that's like hiring outside consultants to study a market. It's never as good as doing it yourself."*[11]

Trump understands marketing; whatever he has been able to achieve till date, marketing has played a key role in it. Be it his real estate business or his success in winning the Presidential elections in the United States, he has never shied away from using any platform or any opportunity to market himself. He has used traditional media and social media very cleverly, and till date, the media has not been able to lose interest in him – and he has been able to achieve all this at a fraction of the cost in comparison to what he would have done traditionally. He compelled the media to talk about him and without really advertising himself, was successful in keeping and retaining the spotlight on himself. He is smart enough to understand the power of negative and positive media, and in a very calculated manner, he has manipulated them in constantly talking about him – be it by attacking him or by supporting him. He was very successful in carving out a niche for himself during campaigning; he used the media to widen that niche audience; he spoke what they wanted to hear; he understood his audience well and marketed or pitched himself accordingly.

The Indian administration must be ready with a marketing plan for Trump, and it should build a positive plan so that it is easy for him to play on it. India should be careful, as in the absence of a proper plan or a properly chalked-out strategy, she will provide a free run to the American President to say anything – which may prove to be too expensive for both the administrations.

It is important that proper marketing capsules are created and shared at all levels of the Trump administration so that there is confidence in them about the Indian position and strategy.

Apart from intensifying and expanding the diplomatic relationship with the United States, other initiatives like trade meets and fairs should be organised on a fast track to exchange and build on opportunities for both the nations. These should be widely publicised and marketed. The perception of American business houses and common American citizens should be built positively and constructively. This should be done by emphasising on the role that Indians and Indian companies have played in creating many more job opportunities for Americans than the Mexican, Canadian or Chinese companies in the United States of America. Indian immigrants and Indian companies have founded more engineering and technology companies in the United States than immigrants from the UK, China, Taiwan and Japan combined. Unlike Mexico, the immigrants from India are generally well-educated and well-trained. The myth of Indians taking away American jobs needs to be proven wrong, and the Indian government must help in shattering this myth.

- A joint Duke University–UC Berkeley study revealed that Indian immigrants have founded more engineering and technology companies from 1995 to 2005 than immigrants from the UK, China, Taiwan and Japan combined.
- A thirdof the Silicon Valley scientists and engineers were immigrants; and that Indians are the second largest group of Asian-born engineers (23%) followed by the Chinese (51%).
- Approximately 7 per cent of high-technology firms in the Silicon Valley were led by Indian CEOs.
- As per the US census statistics, Indian-Americans have attained the highest educational levels in all ethnic groups in the US. Approx. 71 per cent of all Indians have a Bachelor's or higher degree (compared to 28 per cent national and 44 per cent average for all Asian-American groups). Almost 40 per cent of all Indians in the

US have a master's, doctorate, or other professional degrees, which is five times the national average.

- Indian-Americans are generally well-off. The median annual household income for the Indian-Americans in 2010 was US$88,000 – much higher than for all Asian-Americans (US$66,000) and all US households (US$49,800). Only 9 per cent of adult Indian-Americans live in poverty, compared with 12 per cent of Asian-Americans overall and 13 per cent of the US population.
- Approx. 28 per cent of Indian-Americans worked in science and engineering fields; according to the 2013 American Community Survey, more than two-thirds (69.3%) of 16 years and above were in management, business, science and arts occupations.

Indian role models should be identified, and interaction sessions amongst different stakeholders must be initiated on an urgent basis. The quality of Indian goods should be presented in a positive light in comparison with other available options in America.

8. Fight Back

> *"Much as it pays to emphasise the positive, there are times when the only choice is confrontation. In most cases, I'm very easy to get along with. I'm very good to people who are good to me. But when people treat me badly or unfairly or try to take advantage of me, my general attitude, all my life, has been to fight back very hard. The risk is that you'll make a bad situation worse, and I certainly don't recommend this approach to everyone. But my experience is that if you're fighting for something you believe in—even if it means alienating some people along the way—things usually work out for the best in the end."*[12]

Trump has been combatant with the media; his constant duel with the media still continues. All through his election campaign and the time that he has put in office, he has been taking on his opponents aggressively. He has been taunting media with adverbs like "fake news"; his administration is fighting legal battles on many of his executive orders in various courts in America. So, it can be taken that he would not hold himself to any restraint if antagonised, and that he is going to be assertive on his expectations.

There are many sticky points between India and the United States of America, and Trump has very strong views and perceptions on those. He has been expressing his views on the H1B visas as well as on the trade imbalance with India. Those perceptions would have to be softened as suggested earlier; however, it is very much possible that he may continue with his viewpoint. In such a scenario, Indian exports might suffer. India should be well-prepared for this, and must have a plan in case such a scenario plays out.

It is in India's interest to have a strategic relationship with the United States in order to thwart an aggressive China and hostile Pakistan, yet she will have to wait and watch how Trump handles the United States' relationship with China and Pakistan. All through his campaign, he has been promising on taking on China; he has promised to ensure corrective stringent measures against the currency manipulation undertaken by China to support the Chinese exports artificially. Till now, Trump has not taken any significant step towards the same. There seems to be no change in the American policy till now towards China. Although he had issued executive orders on NAFTA and the cancellation of TPPA as he promised in his poll campaign, a similar aggression is missing against China, which he was demonstrating earlier while campaigning. He has been contradictory to his stated stand on a number of occasions with China, and instead oftaking a tough stand on the country, he seems to be moving closer to China. It's to be seen whether there is a change in his viewpoint,if he is following the previous government's trade policy for China, or if there is some other compulsion.

India must look for consistency in the new American President's policy towards China before she commits herself to any trade deal with Trump, and she must be wary of any American attempt to project India against China. India should be ready to call the bluff in such a scenario. Trump was upset with China over the way it played the global trading system in its favour and also by the misuse of the IPR. As President-elect, he even questioned the 'One-China Policy' and took a call from the Taiwanese Prime Minister as a direct snub to China. However, he retracted to the stated American policy and reaffirmed the American commitment to the stated policy of 'One-China'. The Chinese President had refused to take his call, unless the new President clarified this ambiguity. This was the first diplomatic victory for China. Trump's refusal to name China as the currency manipulator and not being fair in trade was another victory for China. Moreover, now Trump is seeking China's help in keeping North Korea in check, which further weakens Trump's stand against China. There is too much oscillation between what he says and his deeds, and it has been a completely muddled-up approach till now. And so, it is best to wait and let the dust settle.

The onus of safeguarding India's trade interests is on the Indian government; and for that, it must be ready to fight it out at all levels – the contingency plans need to be ready with different approaches and multiple strategies. Rather than being reactive, India should be proactively prepared. As stated earlier, America needs access to the Indian market as much as we need access to theirs; hence any misadventure by America is going to severely hurt it too. India should be ready to fight it out.

For the Indian exporters, they will have to be ready to fight the competition out by improving their quality, timely deliverables, innovation, improving productivity, bringing in cost efficiencies and new management practices. There cannot be any substitute to them.

9. Deliver the Goods

> *"You can't con people, at least not for long. You can create excitement, you can do wonderful promotion and get all kinds of press, and you can throw in a little hyperbole. But if you don't deliver the goods, people will eventually catch on."*[13]

As a realtor and successful businessman, Trump understood the value of fulfilling the promises made to the customers. His attempt has been to exceed the expectation of his mentors. Having said this, he is still far away from coming closer to the promises he has made. He is yet to come up with any concrete plan or policy. The action taken till now is very little, and that too, not without hiccups and generating controversies.

His protectionist and narrow view about America is not winning him any new allies; in truth, all his trade-related actions and statements have helped China. He has alienated the US from its strategic allies and trade partners. His cancellation of the TPP and relook into NAFTA, his insistence on building up the wall, his immigration policy – all have been helpful to only one nation, i.e. China, a nation against which he complained of being unfair and labelled'manipulator of currency'. His actions are contrary to his stated goals.

He is still relatively new to his role and it is very much possible that in some more time, he would be able to articulate his views and the direction of his policy in more clear terms. It's very much possible that he is deliberately trying to stir the world, making his allies understand not to take America for granted and putting doubts into the minds of his adversaries. He may be trying to test the waters before jumping in.

It would be in India's interest to let the dust settle as there is no point rushing in a brewing storm. Ultimately, Trump will have to deliver the goods to the American citizens.

The American market is the biggest one for Indian goods and service exports, hence any negative impact there is certainly going to adversely impact Indian exports. The onus lies on the Indian exporters and the Indian government to get their act together and create such a proposition that it becomes difficult for Trump's administration to ignore them. The Indian government can engage with Trump's administration and use its leverage, through government-to-government procurement deals and by lowering trade barriers. If the Trump administration still looks elsewhere, then the loss is theirs and they can continue to strengthen China's trade at the cost of American and Indian interests.

10. Contain the Costs

"I believe in spending what you have to. But I also believe in not spending more than you should. When I was building low-income housing, the most important thing was to get it built quickly, inexpensively and adequately so you could rent it out and make a few bucks. That's when I learned to be cost-conscious. I never threw money around. I learned from my father that every penny counts, because before too long, your pennies turn into dollars.

> *To this day, if I feel a contractor is overcharging me, I'll pick up the phone, even if it's only for $5,000 or $10,000, and I'll complain. People say to me, "What are you bothering for over a few bucks?" My answer is that the day I can't pick up the telephone and make a twenty-five-cent call to save $10,000 is the day I'm going to close up shop.*
>
> *The point is that you can dream great dreams, but they'll never amount to much if you can't turn them into reality at a reasonable cost.*"[14]

As a businessman, this is the most important characteristic of Trump. He understands profits, and he understands the role of costs in maximising his profits. Just because you have enough money or resources, it is not a reason for you to burn it out. He is willing to extend himself to save that one dollar for himself. His approach is not going to be different when he would be expected to resolve the American trade issues. He would not hesitate to move away from conventional wisdom or backtrack if he feels that a particular route or approach to protecting American interests is going against it. This can be seen in the context of his dealings with or his approach to China, Russia, Canada and the UK, where he has been unconventional and not hesitated from taking a contrary stand on either the previous government policy or, for that matter, what he himself had been stating in his election campaigns.

His being vocal about the issues related to bad deals like NAFTA or TPPA, or with Japan and China, is nothing short of his attempt to contain the costs.

India, too, has much to work on this aspect. The Indian government will have to put in serious thoughts on opening the Indian market to American companies, if India wishes to have a far greater access to the American market. At least with Trump, it seems a distant possibility that India would be able to gain any major share in the American market unless she sweetens the deal for Trump. And according to me, there is tremendous scope for India to sweeten the deal.

India must look within to improve its infrastructure and export policy to encourage more exports. The price advantage that China has is not only because of its currency manipulation, but is also driven largely by the infrastructure that it has put in place to encourage manufacturing and exports. The Chinese have been able to edge out tough competition not only by maintaining quality standards, but by providing products at the most cost-efficient pricing. The government policies and infrastructure play a large role in the final cost of the product.

Power, land, transportation and logistics, customs, finance costs, labour laws, insurance and taxation are all under the government domain, and its share in the overall production cost is as much as 100 per cent (if considered also for incremental costs on other services required for production) of the actual production cost. The same is true for all sorts of exports – be it goods or services. Just because the services export is growing at a much faster pace, it is no reason for the Indian companies and government to be complacent, as their current business models are already being challenged and profitability is dropping.

The Indian government can help Indian exporters and manufacturers by creating and providing the basic infrastructure and improving on transportation and logistics. Simplifying taxes, customs and other paperwork required for promoting exports from India is necessary. The labour laws also need to be reformed in line with new realities and a balance needs to be generated. The government policy towards the Ministry of Micro Small and Medium Enterprises (MSME) entities and their role in exports also needs to be addressed and modified. At times, the good intentions of the government itself turn into a major roadblock as the policy may be acting as a barrier for large corporate houses to produce through their excess capacity for exports.

Similarly, the Indian exporters will have to improve upon their attitude towards exports. They will have to move from the lower end of the value chain to the upper end. They will need to bring in new technologies and increase their productivity levels. The Indian exporter has got into the habit of hiding behind the government, and is dependent on doles of the government to push exports. They will have to not only adapt but will have to innovate, invest in R&D and improve on their quality. They will have to match their commitments and export obligations in time. Price certainly is an important aspect of the business and too much depends on it; however, price is not the only winning factor. The Indian exporters have too much to learn, and unless they don't accept this and improve their standards, the Indian exports segment will go through a difficult time ahead.

11. Have Fun

> *"Money was never a big motivation for me, except as a way to keep score. The real excitement is playing the game.*
>
> *It never stops, and I wouldn't have it any other way. I try to learn from the past, but I plan for the future by focusing exclusively on the present. That's where the fun is. And if it can't be fun, what's the point ?"*[15]

"Fun" is being high on challenges and desire to resolve them and doing what the others thought was undoable. Fun is in taming a wild horse and riding it. Fun is in breaking the convention and getting the results which were unachievable, working out new strategies, innovating and doing something really great. Trump has already booked his date with the history of America; he has already achieved something which many considered impossible. He proved his detractors wrong when they had already written his political obituaries; he took on the challenge from being a distant outsider to becoming the central fulcrum and won. That's where the fun began, and it has just begun for him.

India, too, can enjoy the ride and have fun working along as a team. Trump enjoys getting personal and trying to know people he is going to work with. He enjoys spending time and sharing his experiences, sharing a good time with his counterparts. He tries to get a measure of the person he is going to deal with, so spending time with him is going to be crucial. Making deals while having fun is an approach he enjoys and deploys.

Trump has made it amply clear that he is against multilateral agreements; Trump feels that in such agreements, America ends up paying and becomes a loser in the end. He does not believe in globalization; he is more for a bilateral approach, where a calibrated path can be laid between the two parties and deals brokered easily and fast.

This approach is suitable for India as she, too, hesitates in committing or investingherself in multilateral agreements. India, apart from the WTO, is not part of any major multilateral trade agreement. The Indian political system and administration is very wary of foreign intervention in Indian affairs. That her past colonial masters took the route of trade to make India its colony is still fresh, hence every trade deal is evaluated and re-evaluated.

END NOTES

1. *The Art of the Deal* (1987) by Donald J. Trump.
2. *The Art of the Deal* (1987)
3. *The Art of the Deal* (1987)
4. *The Art of the Deal* (1987)
5. https://www.nytimes.com/2014/12/12/opinion/let-india-make-cheap-drugs.html?_r=0
6. https://www.theguardian.com/sustainable-business/patent-wars-india-takes-on-big-pharma
7. *The Art of the Deal* (1987)
8. http://www.livemint.com/Politics/H9mJDSrD7DZStOeF8BLcaN/India-now-3rd-largest-aviation-market-in-domestic-air-passen.html
9. http://www.boeing.co.in/news-and-media-room/news-releases/2016/july/boeing-forecasts-demand-for-1850-new-airplanes-in-india.page?
10. *The Art of the Deal* (1987)
11. *The Art of the Deal* (1987)
12. *The Art of the Deal* (1987)
13. *The Art of the Deal* (1987)
14. *The Art of the Deal* (1987)
15. *The Art of the Deal* (1987)

SECTION TWO

PATIENCE IS A VIRTUE

Foreign trade isn't easy. Most successful international trade businesses reached where they are through hard work, persistence and resolve. There are many angles to foreign trade relationship and business; its architecture is far more complex and invisible than what it seems.

Trump's administration is very vocal on evaluating existing trade agreements, scrapping, re-negotiating or forging new trade agreements from the perspective of safeguarding American exports, generating and retaining employment in America. Trump already has and may even declare some more of them null and void, and pull America out of them. But creating and forging new trade agreements, even though they may be bilateral, is not as easy as it seems. It takes years for a trade agreement to be actually put in action after it's negotiated, ratified and accepted in both the trading countries. International trade agreements are not business deals between two businesses or traders, it involves many other objectives other than business or safely putting in money or economics. Angles like national security, national and international politics, health and social security, climate, job securities and access to critical mineral resources are part of it.

With the stated policy of Trump's administration of America first, it has amply made clear to the other negotiators on the table that it is going to fiercely protect the American interest. This reciprocally and equally means that it is for the other nation to evaluate, check and protect its own interest —and this is where it is tricky and patience is (going to be) a virtue.

The panic that has set in in the international trade circles by statements made by the President of United States or by his administration is not in sync with reality. Trump's administration has managed to shock the world with its unconventionalities, but it is far from changing anything worthwhile internationally. Except for low-hanging fruits, the Americans have not been able to pluck anything worthwhile. Pulling out of the TPPA is not going to make any impact on the world trade currently as the treaty was yet to be ratified by the Congress. It had more of a symbolic value for the American citizens and businesses; it was more for political benefit and grand-standing than economy. And the deal was as good as a dead snake, as the American Congress was yet to ratify and approve it. Similarly, the NAFTA is to be renegotiated between Canada and Mexico. The provisions for periodic negotiations were already a part of the treaty and like America, Mexico and Canada also had been facing certain heat domestically, where their trade interests were hurting due to American exports. Renegotiation also gives them an equal opportunity to plug in the holes where it is hurting the Mexican and Canadian interests.

> *The NAFTA renegotiations won't begin for at least another three months and according to Commerce Secretary Wilbur Ross, will take at least a year – if not more. Mr Ross says mildly that NAFTA 'needs an update' and the negotiation may produce 'marginal benefits' for the United States – a modest and probably accurate assessment. After discussion with the administration this month, Mexico's foreign minister told reporters there had been 'no talk of unilateral action'.*[1]

Obituaries about free trade, globalisation and liberalisation of trade have been written, without deeply analysing or checking on actions yet to be enacted by the Trump administration. Two months into his Presidency, Trump has not been able to achieve much or disturb the world order, other than isolating America from the world and providing opportunity to China and the EU to fill in the vacuum caused. By discontinuing the policy of the previous Obama administration, Trump has been successful in derailing the efforts put in by the previous American administration for the last decade or so, and providing opportunity to China to step into its shoes, especially in the Asian context. In all probability, it is possible that President Trump may do a complete flip over on China later, when it dawns on him that trade ties and economies are far more integrated and complex, and any adverse action by America unilaterally is going to weaken its own economy and trade. It is one thing to be vocal and spewing rhetoric about keeping "American interest first" but in a true sense, to keep the American interest first is another thing when its economy is dependent on cheaper and competitive imports from other nations. Any misadventure is only going to cause an imbalance in the American economy and trade.

India should be patient enough and not give into knee-jerk reactions to these statements or situations. The hard reality is that India has little to lose and much to gain if it is persistent enough to carefully analyse the situation, plan well and engage with Trump's administration in a constructive and balanced manner.

The advantage that India has is that it can clear its slate and redraft the trade engagements with the United States. India, unlike the United States of America, has been wary of signing multilateral trade treaties and has been very cautious about committingherself to many of the multilateral or multinational trade agreements that are in vogue – till the time Trump took the United States of America away from them. Trump and his administration wish to forge new trade treaties on bilateral terms, which suits and matches the approach taken by India.

Patience shall not be mistaken for no action or misunderstood as is ordinarily-put, "Wait & Watch". Nowhere is it being suggested that the Indian government should continue on the same path that it's presently taking, and neither has it been suggested that there should be an abrupt change in that path. Patience herein means being ready for action when the timing is correct. This in a true sense means that India needs to introspect, realign and put herself on a trajectory wherein she is able to benefit herself when the time for trade negotiations comes. India should not wait for the storm to come and create havoc, but plan on how to contain the negative impact, harness its energy and turn it into an opportunity for herself.

If we carefully analyse and do a reality check, India and America bilaterally have much to gain from the existing situation. They both play a complementary role to each other's needs, and if played well, both the Trump administration as well as the Modi government can successfully fulfil their objectives. The strengthening of trade ties between the two nations itself can be a game-changer in the world. "India needs America as much as America needs India"–if this reality is accepted open-mindedly in political, economic and trade circles of both the nations, it can boost job growth and take both nations on to a progressive path. India and America, though different in many aspects, have much more in common and far more greater potential than any of the existing trade partners of America. However, that true potential has never been able to be professed, and is lacking in a correct review of the situation, commitment and engagement at both ends. The current scenario presents India and America with a chance to renew and form a new economic strategic partnership–a win–win situation for both.

As per my observation and carefully trying to read between the lines of the 2017 Trade Agenda set by President Trump, it seems that his intention is actually to reduce the trade deficits between the US and its trading partners. To me, when the Trump administration mentions fair play in trade, it means that it expects the trading partners to open up their markets for American goods and services, and therein lies a unique opportunity for India and America – as India needs American investments, goods and services in multiple priority areas like infrastructure, defence, aviation, smart cities, sanitation, energy etc., where she needs the technological as well mechanical inputs from America; and there lies an opportunity for America to increase its export share to India and reduce its trade deficit. Similarly, the urgent requirement in the US is to shift its dependence on Mexico, Canada and China for many of the goods and services that these nations fulfil and provide to the US. India can, and has, the potential to step into their shoes, provided the Indian government and the American administration are able to gauge this opportunity and are able to mutually work around bilateral trade treaties.

Patiently, India will have to work at multi-platforms, and will have to segregate the nibbling political issues from the economical ones. The current superficial relationship would need to be more meaningful and further strengthened by spending more time with each other – both at a senior political level and simultaneously at the administration level, with other stakeholders like civil society and business representatives.

There are a number of hurdles that both the Trump administration as well as the Indian government will have to cross. Many of these hurdles are decades-old and lie in the foundation of the Indo-American historical engagements. Although the United States of America had been a supporter of the Indian freedom struggle, yet their relationship till date has been bumpy – havingseen many highs and lows. The situation is complex when the United States tries to equate or balance India with Pakistan, China or Russia. The burden of the past would need to be completely lifted so that a new relationship of mutual trust and respect can breathe.

The impediments in the Indo-US relations can be listed as:

- Mutual trust and respect deficiency
- Disappointment in establishment and achievement of major short-term objectives
- Lack of a true understanding of bilateral economic activities and their potential
- Absence of meaningful ideas, which are pragmatic and can be realistically applied

Most Americans are still suffering from the symptoms of "the Chained Elephant". Despite all the progress that India has made till date: when India is the third largest economy of the world with the development growth rate being highest in the world; when Indians have successfully launched and completed the Mars mission at a fraction of the cost of any American space programme – still, to many Americans, India is a land of snake charmers and a country of illiterate and the poor. This is not to dispute that India is struggling in providing many of the basic necessities to its citizens, and that both urban and rural India still have to go a long way to match the level of the developed nations, this is precisely the prospect that the American companies and American government can win over. This is the space in which the current Indian government is inviting the investments for helping build a new developed and infrastructurally strong India. This is the opportunity for American service providers, especially in engineering, technology, finance, healthcare etc.

Another big weakness in the India–US bilateral relationship is when it comes to strategic issues, India and the US become confrontationist and don't see eye-to-eye. In many of the international forums, America is seen as force-aligning and representing the interest of the rich, developed and manipulating nations, and India is seen as representing the interests of poor, developing and suffering nations. Quite often, America and India have been at the two ends of the spectrum.

The US administration fails to recognise that India has a mind of its own. From the time it became independent, it has been very cautious in its approach – especially while dealing with the West. Trade was the route that its former colonial rulers took to make India a British colony, and as it happened with every other colony, India suffered a lot economically, socially, culturally, racially and politically. It has a deep mistrust of this approach, and is ultra-sensitive while dealing with the West and developed nations in general. The founding fathers of the nation charted a non-aligned route for India and maintained an equal distance between the two Cold War-era power centres. The foreign policy of India has been to resist getting embroiled in any kind of conflict. India, traditionally, except for the UN, has never been part of any security bloc like the NATO; neither has it allowed its territory for being used for any kind of armed base for foreign countries or allies. Politically, Indians are very sensitive to any kind of alignment with a Western military power.

The gap has widened due to India's boundary conflict with Pakistan and China, and the United States' aligning itself with Pakistan during the Indo-Pak wars. This is, till date, etched in the minds and hearts of Indians. And in the current context with the US engaged in conflict in Afghanistan, it has been dependent on Pakistan for logistical support to its troops. Unfortunately, till date, neither India nor the US has been able to look beyond the prism of Pakistan. The US perceives that if it has to further its trade relationship with India, then India must also become its strategic ally in the Asian context. This is not acceptable to India. And India believes that the US has been biased against it since 1947, when it started backing Pakistan and led to many sanctions being imposed on India. The sanctions imposed on India after the nuclear tests conducted in Pokharan, again, were adversarial and still fresh in the memory of Indians. India wishes America to value its relationship in an independent manner, without pushing India into any corner or directly linking it with Pakistan or China.

Although the relationship has moved and progressed in recent years, there is a lot to desire. The goals of the Trump administration for protecting and advancing American interests, and that of the Indian government to expand the export base in America and inviting American investments into India, can only be fulfilled if both the nations work on respecting and trusting each other. The true depth of the trade relationship depends upon how deep the trust develops amongst the two nations, and how fundamentally strong their foundations are.

If the Indian and the US government wish to pursue and push the trade ties and take a big leap, then instead of focusing on the political agenda, they need to move on to an economic partnership. In the absence of any deep economic foundation, the possibility of strategic partnership is diluted and staggered, and it would be similar to climbing a one-legged ladder that's guaranteed to fail. An outdated defensiveness and aggressiveness in trade negotiations must give way to pragmatism and new resolve. The attitude of both, the government and the administration, must change towards each other, and a deeper understanding and respect must evolve towards geopolitical, economic and security limitations.

The Indian and American governments need to be tolerant and aligned to the boundaries that can be stretched or simply not touched. Hard posturing, sanctions, threats or non-alignment is not going to give the desired results. The US government and policymakers must understand and reframe the terms they use in crafting a partnership with a rising India that does not strive for an alliance relationship with the United States. And similarly, it is important for the Indian government to understand that it can't continue to stand on the sidelines on international geopolitical and economic developments and events occurring in the world. It will have to get proactively involved and sit on the high table, get involved in policy drafting, setting the ground rules and leading – rather than being passive and later finding loopholes or holding a divergent view, when the world has moved in other direction. This passiveness or late somersault behaviour frustrates Americans, and is of no good to India.

India and the Trump administration have a golden chance to forge a bilateral Free Trade Agreement (FTA), where clear terms can be set to safeguard the interests of both the nations. This needs an urgent push and the Indian government should be ready with its set of priorities and solutions for genuine American concerns. For India, not only is it important to expand its export base, but equally important to increase imports from the US as well. Our belief is that this can be simultaneously balanced at both ends, and both the nations can be winners. The American businesses need the Indian market, and the Indian government can channelise this through establishing government-to-government procurement and trade agreements, especially for sectors like aviation, railways, defence, shipbuilding, smart cities infrastructure, communications, energy, sanitation, fuel, insurance, education, healthcare, construction, oil exploration, etc. These are sectors wherein the Indian government plays a crucial role, and by modifying and moving away from a standard procurement process to a more strategic inter-governmental trade relationship, not only would it enable the Indian government to attract American businesses but also provide a way-out to the Trump' administration to balance the trade deficit that America presently views as a major concern.

Both the nations can also take up joint development and co-production by mapping and analytically selecting the core strengths in each of the nations. Inter-governmental agreements can take care of the IPR concerns and ensure that both nations' interests are well-protected. Pharmaceuticals, defence, mobile and communication equipment, healthcare, and power andenergy are certain sectors where the possibility of joint development and co-production in the two nations seem realistic and promising.

India has an advantage in low costs for labour-intensive export sectors; its geographical location, size and numerous climatic zones are ideal for agricultural and horticultural produce. Sectors like apparels and clothing, leather, fisheries and aquaculture, food grains and other agricultural products, food processing, etc. could be certain sectors where America can cooperate and benefit from the Indian exports to it. Trade conflict can be avoided by listing out the sectors or product categories, where the interests of the American farmers can be simultaneously protected.

Similarly, in the service sectors, Indians need to move on from a lower base of service offerings like BPOs to innovative new solutions by developing new programmes, software and physical infrastructure. The IT sector is another big opportunity for American businesses to set-up joint R&D centres, software development labs, cloud-computing hubs, digital studios for gaming, entertainment etcetera. India can be the American route for creating an "emerging market product and services innovation hub", and benefit from India's proximity to the Asian and African nations. Terms to protect the intellectual property rights and to prevent privacy can be stringently put in the FTA. The IPR is one of the key issues between India and the US trade relationship, and would need urgent attention now. India will have to demonstrate its clear intent to the US, and must be more committed to it. Similarly, the US would have to understand the limitations of India as it cannot be sightless to the challenges that India faces.

Clearly, the American space programmes and their knowledge and intelligence is way ahead of India. Yet, India has proven through its own space programmes that it has the capability to develop and implement technology which is a fraction of the cost in comparison to the American programmes. The Indian satellite launches and the Mars mission are living examples. America and India can gain from each other's experience by joining hands. Not only will America be able to save huge costs, but will be able to provide high-end technology and equipment. It can gain from India's frugal approach.

India will have to work in tandem with the American foreign trade policymakers to ensure that no unnecessary trade barriers are put across in the two nations, and that any genuine issues are mutually/bilaterally sorted out on priority. The trade barriers hindering trade in both nations need to be brought down.

There are many measures that the Indian government and other stakeholders can take immediately without waiting to establish and safeguarding the exports of Indian goods and services. They need to be prepared and must have a lobbying plan to create support for Indian products. The Indian trade representative in the Indian mission in the US should be proactive and participate in constructive campaigning.

India must hire specialists in America to guide and create a policy framework and guidelines for India to handle and meet the sanitary and photo-sanitary standards and conditions, so that Americans can be guaranteed that their standards would be matched. Training modules should be created to bring awareness and to train Indian businesses and exporters on American standards and expectations. This is the least expensive mode of preparing Indian businesses to increase Indian exports and its acceptance by the American citizens. This would also help in increasing an Indian exports base in theEU and other developed nations.

India must have an aggressive marketing plan for Indian products, and must support and advertise to create a positive aura around the Indian goods and services. The compliance with American standards must enhance the confidence of the American consumers for Indian products and services. Similarly, an equal push needs to be undertaken in India on merits, awareness and compliance certification and authentication to ensure that there is no rejection of Indian products, which till now has the highest rejection rate for exported goods amongst all nations to the US. The major reasons for the rejection of Indian products are listed below, which if analysed, could have been easily avoided. The rejections have been for the following reasons:

- Non-compliance with American quality standards
- Wrong labelling and misbranding
- Wrong packaging
- Pollutants and high residual levels
- Contamination or found to be unhygienic while being tested
- Adulteration
- Unapproved or unacceptable products

The setting-up of a chain of third party laboratories, expert in American standards and in complying with international quality checking, auditing, monitoring and certification processes can help overcome many of the rejections listed above. The same agencies can undertake quality checks for materials, production processes, environmental concerns, compliance to sanitary and phytosanitary conditions and branding and packaging. Many international firms are already providing such services at the international level. The Indian government must encourage such international quality audit organisations to set-up their base in India. Such firms also have a good understanding of international trade laws.

The Indian government must also encourage the setting-up of such Indian laboratories and quality audit firms. Institutes and training programmes must be formulated and aggressively promoted in India. Currently, Indian businesses have to struggle in this aspect as there is a serious crunch of qualified or well-trained quality auditors.

An ease of doing business in India has received a push from the current government, and some positive results are showing; however, the gap is still too large and many more strong steps would need to be undertaken by the government. India's ranking in the ease of doing business list is dismally low, and reflects the huge challenges that the domestic as well as multi-national manufacturers and service providers have to face. The challenges in the ease of doing business are not purely infrastructural, but also related to services that are abysmally slow-paced or obstructionist in outlook.

For foreign trade to increase, a relook into the Indian trade policy is required. The processes and infrastructure around the trade life cycle need to be revisited and simplified. Though ICEGATE (E-Commerce portal of Central Board of Excise and Customs)has been put into use, and has reduced many of the problems earlier faced by traders; it needs to be further upgraded and many of the loose ends need to be resolved. The system and process of customs duty calculations, shipment valuation, etc. should be more transparent and simplified.

The Indian import policy needs to be re-engineered and modified to remove many of the conflicting and confusing points not only for the American imports into India, but for imports from the other nations as well. The business organisations from the United States have actively sought bilateral and multilateral opportunities to India's market, and the government of India has undertaken, and is further pursuing ongoing economic reforms. Nonetheless, the US exporters in many sectors encounter tariff and non-tariff barriers that impede the imports of US products into India, with no conscious advantage to it; on the contrary, they work against India's interests. A clarity in the import policy needs to be brought in, and such barriers need to be altogether eliminated or reduced. Few of the sectors which the Government of India shall consider opening up to the American firms should be architecture, engineering, entertainment andaudio-visual services, telecommunications, accounting, American universities and education institutes, etc. Any concern that both the governments have would need to be tackled across the board, and in a time-bound manner.

The time is opportune for India to be proactive at its own end to tie the loose ends and to patiently move and seal an FTA with the Trump administration, and set aside any differences. The Trump administration would be equally interested in capturing the opportunity to create a balance, and reduce its dependence on China, Mexico and Canada.

END NOTES

1. https://www.lowyinstitute.org/the-interpreter/global-economy-surviving-trump-just-fine

Section Three

Need for Action

Increasing Indian exports in America when the President of the United States is banking on increased protectionism, nationalism and balancing trade deficits with its trade partner (where America already has a trade deficit with India) requires a realignment and modification of the Indian export policies and approach.

In view of the above, India has to take a holistic overview of its approach to exports as a whole, identify the gaps and plug them. And rather than relying on the crutches of incentives and sops, the exporters must take on the opportunities on the pillars of quality, design, cost efficiency, committed timelines and fairness.

The time is opportune for India to dwell upon and take a 360-degree view to strengthen and build its manufacturing and export base. Manufacturing and exports are directly proportional; hence, every attempt would need to be put across to increase the manufacturing capacity, and an increase in exports is a logical outcome to it.

Following are few of the suggestions and recommendations on urgent actions that the Indian government needs to initiate. Many of these suggestions are not new as they have been in the knowledge of the Indian government; some action also already been taken on a few of them, but still, it is critical to list them again as the government still needs to cover a long distance. The government has still not aligned to the belief that to increase the manufacturing and exports base, a more holistic view on policy needs to be undertakenbecause bits and pieces of action here and there are not going to bring about any considerable results. Unless all the stakeholders do not act in a planned and coordinated manner, no major outcome can be expected. The success of programmes like "Make in India" and "Digital India" is not possible unless the entire government machinery acts in unison —including the state governments, manufacturer associations, exports and trade bodies and other stakeholders, including labour unions, etc.

SUGGESTIONS AND RECOMMENDATIONS

1. Market Mapping

a) State-wise

American market mapping, analysis and creation of a data bank for raw produce, consumer and capital goods and for services export need to be put in place. The updated information on the same should be available online to Indian exporters. The information should be collated in a manner that is easy to cross-reference, and is actionable. It should be a precise, ready reckoner with customised services to exporters for their queries, and the support required that is specific to America.

Indian exporters have to struggle when it comes to trade data and its analysis. The data currently provided on various Indian sites is in sharp contrast with each other, and cannot be reliably depended upon. The United States of America has 50 states, with a population of 324 million, and is the third largest country in the world. It is the largest importer in the world. The consumption pattern in each of the 50 states is different, and has different requirements to be fulfilled. The Census Bureau of the United States of America publishes annual figures on each of the 50 states' international trade. It records the top 25 goods imported and exported from each state; the Census Bureau also reports the 25 countries that each state imports the most from and exports the most to. China, Canada and Mexico dominate in respective states. Approximately, 23 of the American states are dominated by Canada; around 18 states are dominated by China, 3 states by Mexico, 3 by Germany and 1 each by India, South Korea and Saudi Arabia. China's share in the American imports is around 22 per cent,

Canada around 13 per cent and Mexico around 12.9 per cent; and India is around merely 2 per cent. What is interesting to note is that Canada, with a 13 per cent market share, is the dominant import partner for 23 states, and Mexico with a similar share is a dominant import partner to just 3 states – that, too, which are closer to the Mexican border. China is evenly spread out across America, whereas India's presence is on the eastern side only. India is within the top 10 countries that rank as importing partners for 23 states and in top 5 countries that are ranked in 4 states. This, when compared with China, Canada and Mexico, is dismal as they are in the top 5 ranks in all the 50 states.

This requires serious planning from the Indian administration if it intends to capture some considerable market share in the US. It will have to map each of these 50 states and identify the export opportunity for the Indian exporters; it will have to work its strategy around focused states and focused export sectors. One of the ways to categorise the 50 states would be to group them as:

- *Hot Spots:* These could be the states where India ranks in the top 5 as America's import partner. The chances of pushing exports in these states would be considerably high as there is already a certain level of acceptance in the market. These states shall act as fresh launch pads for new Indian opportunities.
- *Warm Spots:* These could be the next 10 states, where India should aim at ranking among the top 15 America import partners. India would need to concentrate really hard on these states as they offer the potential to increase the Indian products in these states. These should be developed as landing pads; it means the emphasis would have to be on increasing the Indian export companies' presence in these states. This would require special attention by the Indian government and the Indian mission in the US.
- *Cold Spots:* These would be the balance of states, where India has stiff competition. These states require special scouting efforts from the Indian government and exporters. They may not be critical to an immediate push in trade, but will play a strong role in the long-term.

b) Sector-wise

Each of the 50 states need to be mapped sector-wise in order to identify which sectors require the imports, what the gap is between demand and supply in those sectors, which country is dominant in each of the sectors in each of the state, and finally, India should list down the sectors or sector in which it can fulfil the gap or edge out competition. Such a data bank would need to be created and an analytical study would have to be undertaken.

Once the actual potential for the Indian exporters is gauged by minutely understanding the states' requirements, the Indian government should craft its policy accordingly and engage with the Trump administration to forge a meaningful trade relationship. An organised, planned and carefully coordinated effort between all stakeholders only will be able to encourage Indian exports in the United States.

The top 5 sectors where India has a presence across the US can be categorised as 'Platinum sectors', the next 10 sectors as the 'Gold sectors' and the next 10 sectors as 'Silver sectors'. India must then check where these sectors stand in their market share in each of the states in the US. The Indian trade bodies must concentrate on increasing their market share in the Silver sector; they need to be aggressively pushed and supported by the Indian government through a policy framework and R&D support. The Platinum and Gold sectors would need thorough assessments, and will need to be guarded as well as expanded to other states where there is a potential for them. They need to be guarded from competition as well as from the American domestic market, which can lobby hard with the American administration to introduce and put new trade barriers. Increasing the fee for H1B visas to discourage the Indian IT market reach in the US is an example of the trade barriers being set-up by the American domestic players as well as the local politicians – in guise of protecting American jobs, of course.

The Indian government and Indian exporters will have to clearly understand the quality, price and service benchmarks. Unless Indian products don't excel in the above, there is little chance that they will be able to garner any additional market share. Although the United States have their own standards for the products and, in general, for the domestic and foreign goods/products or services, they have to match the minimum of those standards; but in addition to the above, the states also have their own laws and standards. A deeper study and understanding of the same has to be undertaken by the Indian government, and must be explained to the Indian manufacturers, service providers and exporters. Compliance and quality benchmarking with the relevant American standards is important, and must be integrated with the Indian manufacturing and exports.

The same is true with environmental and phytosanitary restrictions and compliances. There are states in America where the sensitivity is very high on such considerations, and unless the same are matched, they rally against such imports – and that has a cascading effect on the entire sector in the United States. The Indian manufacturers, producers, service providers and exporters must be well-trained in India in order to understand the necessity to comply with them.

Many of the environmental, phytosanitary and technical standards and conditions are a disguise for implementing trade barriers to discourage imports. These may or may not be country-specific, but they surely are there to protect the local industry or suppliers, and many of them are unjustified and can be challenged. The Indian government should identify such issues and must address them with the American administration. Similarly, the Indian exporters must make the Indian government aware of any such barrier they face.

It is possible to dominate a sector. For example, the Chinese have been able to capture the consumer goods and consumer electronics market in America. So much so that even the American goods produced in America are not able to match their price point. The Chinese have deeply invested in the same, and have studied it well; they have developed their products according to American standards and issue a compliance certificate for the same. Similarly, Indians have been able to dominate a majority of service imports to America, especially for business processing and back-end operations. The reason for the same lies in India being able to support the market by the same service level as expected by the American companies.

English as a language is also an important tool along with the booming IT industry in India. The idea is to carefully analyse the requirements of the sector and match it; unless such gap analysis are undertaken and efforts made through creating proper infrastructure and human resources for the same, increasing Indian exports will be a tough task. Such gap analysis cannot be undertaken by exporters – the Indian government and various Indian export trade bodies will have to invest in such initiatives.

The Indian service exports is currently focused on providing BPO support, and that too by placing or providing outsourced resources; this model of exports has lived out its life and there is already a backlash against this model. It is critical that the Indian IT service sector exports move from the bottom-end of the value chain of low-tech to the upper end of the value chain that is high-tech. This is possible by innovation in the existing service models by providing services from India itself by not needing to station any resources in America. There are new management systems, cloud computing systems, workstation sharing systems, etc., through which Indians from India can provide services to American clients. Similarly, establishing an R&D base in America can help the Indian exporters identify new opportunities, design new software and computing systems which can also address the concerns of the American administration, and add jobs in America itself. The talent pool in the Indian companies can help tracking opportunities and be the flag-bearer for furthering the Indian service penetration in the existing and newer markets.

Other service export sectors like tourism and travel, engineering and architec-tural services, medical and wellness tourism, data analytics, entertain-ment and recreation, content design and creation, animation and FX, etc. also need to be explored for further collaboration and exports from India.

Currently, India ranks eighth amongst the top t10 exporters of services in the world. Technology, innovation, creativity and speed of delivery are rapidly redefining services, as digitisation and the Internet has helped in collapsing distances, and helped the Indian exporters provide solutions and services to their clients in the US. What is critical is that the stakeholders, investors and policymakers are up-to-date with the current statistics in the Indian services landscape to be best equipped thereafter in strategising for the future, and in tapping the American market.

Sector mentors and product category experts must be engaged with the task to promote and bring awareness about Indian capabilities. The government should help create a marketing plan and engagement forums and exhibitions in India as well as in the United States to showcase Indian expertise.

c) Product-wise

Each of the sectors has some hero products which constitute the majority of share in the sector imports in various states of the US. These products have to be identified and evaluated against similar Indian products or product categories. The gaps in quality, pricing, compliances, packing, etc. would have to be minutely analysed. The benchmarking exercises would have to be undertaken.

The top 25 products in each of the top 10 sectors for all states must be listed. Experts must be hired to undertake R&D in these top 25 product categories to help the Indian manufacturers and exports develop products at par, or far superior, than they already are in the American market. Not only would it be beneficial in capturing some American markets, but would also help India raise its quality bar in the domestic markets as well as other developed export markets around the world.

All the data collected and analysed scientifically would open new frontiers for the Indian exporters. The areas where India has potential get missed in the absence of a proper data base to support them. Data is the foundation of strategy, of marketing, for R&D and to understand the gaps. Data gives birth to innovation, and unveils new strengths which could have been hidden till now. Data is the proof that one needs to quantify success or failure. Data analytics and its simplification for the Indian manufacturers and exporters is an important task that the Indian government and Indian trade bodies will have to undertake, if they wish to see the Indian exports rise. They will have to back-up exporters, make it easier for the Indian manufacturers to identify niches for their products in the American markets across states.

2. Radical is the New Normal

Normal won't work...
Conventional approach won't work...
Radical is the new normal...

Since the last three decades, the share of the Indian imports into the United States of America has been flat, with no considerable growth to boast of. Even if we take a closer view, since the year 2010, it has barely risen from 1.6 per cent and is now around 2 per cent of the total American imports. Whereas, in the same period for China, there has been a meteoric rise; its share has risen from 18 to 22 per cent of total American imports.[1]

From 2001 to 2015, imports from China increased dramatically, rising from US$102.3 billion in 2001 to US$462 billion in 2016. In the same period, imports from India to America were US$9.74 billion in 2001 to US$46 billion in 2016.[2] If we compare the growth in percentage terms, one may say that the growth has been similar, but one look at the actual figures clearly demonstrates the huge gap between India's and China's share in the American market. The Chinese market share in the US is 10 times that of India, and catching up to it in a conventional line of approach is not going to win any new markets for India in America.

From an Indian perspective, if we compare the growth in Indian exports to America, we see a steady rise year-on-year at an average rate of 6-7 per cent. Since 2011, the compound growth to date has been around 25 per cent, though that would be a half-truth if seen in growth comparison with China, Canada and other major exporting nations to America. The winner in grabbing the lion's share is China. The existing growth rate of the Indo-American trade would never be able to achieve the target of US$500 billion worth of annual bilateral trade by 2020, as set in the meeting of the American President and the Indian Prime Minister in 2014, though the real potential is twice of the target set and the real target should have been US$ 1trillion by year 2030. China and US bilateral trade is projected to be around US$1.6 trillion by 2022[3] and around US$3 trillion in the same duration. We are barely at 6 per cent of that target, and if we continue with our existing policies and trade practices, we will barely be around 20 per cent of the target – way too short, unless we take a note of it now itself and take corrective steps in the right direction.

The conventional way of forming committees and assigning them the task to suggest and recommend policies within a short duration of time, period, and merely passing on their suggestions and demands to the government is not going to increase Indian exports in America. Similarly, providing further financial incentives to push exports is also not going to get the desired results, These short-cut approaches are like covering a deep wound without a proper understanding of the issues, infections or danger it may cause to the body. It is a knee-jerk reaction. Aggressive export promotions and growth plans need a far more determined, professional and hands-on approach for day-to-day dealing and decision making with the American and Indian administrations.

The government must seriously consider rejigging the existing organisation structure looking after the Indian trade and exports. There are so many commodity boards, so many trade bodies and associations, so many trade councils working towards improving the Indian foreign trade. At the last count, 49 such bodies have been working towards the growth of the Indian trade. The list is attached as Annexure 2. Such bodies not only exist at a Central level, but also at the State(s) level, and furthermore at the sector level. Despite such heavy organisational structures, the result is pretty dismal, and the growth of export continues to fall. The primary reason is that most of these bodies toe the safe line and take the easy way out; for example, demanding more financial incentives for the exporters, demanding to raise more barriers for imports etc., and hence work against the long-term interest of the Indian foreign trade. Instead of just providing incentives and creating barriers, it is more important to create an adequate infrastructure and create more competitiveness. Some of these bodies must be clubbed, and some further expanded with a country-wide presence (for example, the Export Inspection Council) as they play a very important role in guiding and maintaining quality control.

The Indian government must seriously consider creating an empowered apex body (like the USTR) with professionals and top experts/talent hired or identified within the Indian Trade Service officers and Indian Foreign

Service officers – operating on a day-to-day basis, which must guide and lead the trade negotiations and trade agenda. This body shall be well-structured, with a defined organisation chart and goals, a clear captain (who is accountable for the win or loss of the team) and officials with expertise in international trade law, international trade marketing and international commercial and trade practices, along with expert negotiators, research scholars and data analytics. The team can be formed by identifying brilliant talent from various levels of the government and exporters trade associations for the next five to 10 years to ensure continuity and accountability. This body shall be un-biased, full time, non-political, and must be aligned with stiff targets to be achieved. This Apex body shall have professionals well-versed with the Indian manufacturing and trade scenario as well as up-to-date with the American trade scenario. It shall be the coordinating agency for various trade exports promotion bodies and must help strategies, provide direction and resolve issues related to them. It must spearhead at the ground level the tasks of trade negotiations with the American administration, remove trade barriers to Indian exports, challenge unfair practices legally, and create a roadmap for the promotion of Indian products and services in the US.

The Indian government shall put in action an American-centric chapter in the US, by either outsourcing to the local American talent or by deploying a team of officers from the Indian Trade Services. The Indian government can take help from Indians settled and living in the US. There are over 3 million Indian-Americans living in the US, and unlike other Asian immigrants, the American-Indians are evenly spread all across American states. They would help in undertaking extensive market intelligence, build strong launch pads and landing pads for the Indian exporters in different states of America, lobby hard and choose local mentors to promote Indian products and services. The American-Indians are in leadership positions in many of the multinational companies, the government as well as in every service sector or field. Google, Pepsi, Microsoft and many financial institutions and investment banks, engineering, research and design institutions etc. are being led by Indians. The Indian government must seek their help and engage them to create a common platform for Indian products in the US. The top research and analytic modelling companies are based in the US, and many of them are led by Indians or have Indians at important positions. It will be beneficial for India if such organisations are engaged and assigned the task of market intelligence and development of the new matrix and software that help Indian manufacturers/producers and service providers to export their products, in compliance to the American standards and taste. These teams should be given clear goals, and be empowered and backed against any backlash.

3. Create Robust Infrastructure, Logistics and Supply Chain Management

The growth of exports is linked to the growth of manufacturing, and the growth of manufacturing is linked to infrastructure. Even in the service exports, the role of infrastructure cannot be ignored.

Unfortunately, the struggle to provide basic infrastructure still continues in India: power, water, roads, industrial set-up, pollution control facilities, labs, ICD, ports, cold storage, logistics, etc. All these play an important role in bringing down the cost of trade, increase productivity, ensure quality compliance, certification, increase competition as well as reduce the logistical time gaps. The gap between India and other major exporting nations to the United States is tremendous and requires attention at a war footing, if India is serious about increasing its exports share.

• *Power*

The availability of cheap power is the biggest challenge that India faces, as this puts a big dent in manufacturing and production and even service industry suffers due to the shortage of power.[4] And if it is available, the cost of power is one of the highest in India, resulting in over 2-7 per cent of the costs overrun[5] in the entire life cycle of the product being exported, depending upon the electricity consumption for the production/storage of the finished goods. Even 2 per cent is a huge cost difference in international competition, hence it requires urgent attention if the government is keen on increasing manufacturing and exports.

There are power surplus states in India. The power should, on priority, be provided to manufacturing and exports clusters, for this if a separate parallel grid system or a feeder system is to be created, then the same should be undertaken.

Power presents an excellent opportunity for American companies to help India achieve its power requirements, at the same time creating trade opportunities for the American businesses back home. Government-to-government procurement agreements can be undertaken. Special Purpose Venture (SPV) or Vehicle to carry out the objective can be formed, with both the governments being part of it. India has enough experience to protect its interests, and so does America. The SPV shall be accountable for ensuring profitability as well as smooth operations of the system.

The Indian government is aggressive on the smart cities plan, as through that, it wishes to create 100 smart cities. A pilot project on the above lines can be attempted in one of the target cities, and its success will open up many new investment and trade opportunities for both India and America, ranging from engineering, services, IT and manufacturing. The Indian manufacturers would not mind the genuine electricity costs, provided they can be assured of a 24×7 power supply for their industries.

- *Logistics*

The logistics cost in India is around 13 per cent as compared to 8 per cent in China and other major exporting nations. This additional cost of 5 per cent is a big drag on Indian exports. India is at the bottom in terms of its logistics infrastructure rating when compared to the major exporting nations in Asia, and just better than Vietnam and Philippines.[6] One of the key reasons for China's success in capturing the share in exports worldwide and in the US is its transportation and logistical infrastructure. Time is money; every hour saved in the manufacturing cycle is saved in the delivery of finished goods in the market and reduces the pressure on the costs. Not only is the overall productivity better, but the cost efficiency ensures that the manufacturer and exporter remain competitive and are able to guard their market. Transportation and logistics influence every stage of the exports cycle. Logistics encompasses facilities like cold storages and warehouses, packing, loading and unloading infrastructure and services, customs documentation and checking, freight, container depots, tracking infrastructure and devices, etc. Transportation is nowadays part of logistics and clients don't just expect you to deliver at the domestic port, but that the exporters deliver from the source base to the final destination in their country, complete to unloading at their warehouse. The client expects the exporter to keep him updated (real-time) on the status of the delivery. Although there are improvements that have happened within India, yet there is a lot of distance that the government needs to cover and lots of gaps that need to be plugged at every stage of delivery.

It's estimated that the Indian Road Transport Fleet is only effective or productive for 30 per cent of its time.[7] Productive time is lost due to long delays for reasons such as bad roads, jams, check-post inspections, long queues, police etc. The damage or losses due to these delays is between 2-7 per cent, depending upon the perishability of the product being transported. The delays and losses are much higher for the North-East and other states like Uttarakhand, Himachal, and J&K as the terrains are difficult; for states like Jharkhand, Chhattisgarh, Bihar, Odisha, Telengana, etc., the law and order and security issues add to the challenges.

The Indian government should promote the use of modern communication systems and digital technology to help the exporters for a faster clearance on roads for checks, taxation and clearances. The exporters should be able to bill everything online, all taxes, road levies, etc. would be paid online, and such information should automatically get passed on to all the check posts that are en route to the port, from where the material is to be shipped. Mobile phones and Internet network has made faster communication possible in every nook and corner of the country, and the same should help the exporters or logistics management companies to have paperless transit, at least within India. This will help in proper taxation and proper documentation, and will remove corruption and reduce time and cost of transportation.

Imagine that transportation vehicles/container-carrying vehicles are fitted with tracking devices and such authorised devices with RFID from which the government or private toll check posts can extract data, beforehand from a minimum distance of 2 km and clear the vehicle to pass – and if there is any doubt, there are separate stations where a further checking or holding of vehicle can be done. Imagine the container itself being tamperproof and once the custom check would have happened and sealed at the manufacturer or exporter's warehouse, it won't need to be reopened anywhere till it is finally unloaded at its destination. Imagine the ICD depots or the ports having prior information of when the vehicle is going to land in the depot or port so that the vehicles don't have to queue up unnecessarily. Imagine how the productivity of the ports and the ICD will be increased. All this is possible, and is a necessary infrastructure for the exporters to increase their market share in foreign trade.

China, Singapore, Malaysia and Dubai have invested heavily in their logistics infrastructure both within their domestic boundaries as well as internationally. China went to the extent of forging new relationships with its immediate neighbours as well with other friendly countries, by creating a road, rail and port network to reach its export markets. China realises that speed to the market is very important, and if it is able to match speed with further cost efficiency then it doesn't need to worry too much on the future of Chinese exports. China is pursuing the policy of "One Belt, One Road," a policy for the creation of an economic land belt that includes countries on the original Silk Road through Central Asia, West Asia, the Middle East and Europe, as well as a maritime road that links China's port facilities with the African coast. The Chinese have already connected to Europe andthe UK by rail; they have put in action their ambitious plan for reaching the African and West Asian markets through Pakistan, and by a sea route to the Suez Canal.

The priority of the Indian government should be to link the manufacturing hubs and exports clusters to the ICD and ports. A new coastal road network, linking the ports, ICD and export-oriented townships/ clusters for an easy flow of goods, from the raw material to dispatch of finished goods, is necessary. The government should speed up the negotiations with our neighbours for creating a dedicated international road network, through which new trade routes can be opened.

Similar to a loss of time on the roads, the exporters lose considerable time at the ports for reasons like crowding, long queue, checking, customs, etc. The government must push for the fast completion of work as well as the commissioning of work already undertaken on creating eight new ports as well as the modernisation of the existing ports. China has over 34 major ports and over 2,000 mid and small ports, of which around 130 provide access to foreign ships; in comparison India has 12 major and 200 notified minor and intermediate ports. Out of the new ports planned, a selected small or intermediate one could be specific to the US. The infrastructure at this port, personnel training, etc. could be in manner that lessens the time for loading, unloading, custom clearance, quality checks, phytosanitary checks, etc. It should be a facilitator of speedy transfers.

This could be achieved again by creating an SPV and involvement of the two governments or through private investments or FDI. The infrastructure, operations, and maintenance can be undertaken by the SPV, the Indian government can take care of land acquirement and security; the rest is to be provided by the SPV. The focus should be to reduce costs and time along with full capacity utilisation and increasing productivity. The digital initiatives are to be extended to all aspects of port management in order to be paperless and online, removing all chances of corruption and manipulation. Access to American mercantile vessels and other neighbourhood-friendly country vessels can be provided, encouraging a new faster trade route and access into each other's markets.

It is important to create more ICDs linked with railway lines, roads and wherever possible, through river waterways and linked to ports. These ICDs or dry ports can be a boon for landlocked states and states like Uttarakhand, Himachal Pradesh and those of the North-East which have difficult hilly terrain. The ICD will help in faster transportation through dedicated rail or waterway and on-surface transport service providers. This could be achieved through private investments or FDI.

4. Laboratories and Auditing

"From January 2010-December 2015, 13,334 "Made-in-India" items rejected by US-FDA in 6 years; 1,753 less than China.[8]

"*The United States of America rejects Indian shrimps due to antibiotic presence.*"[9] About 88 per cent of the shrimp entry line refusals in May 2016 were from India and were refused due to the presence of banned antibiotics such as Chloramphenicol and Nitrofuran. Both are broad-spectrum antibiotics for human use and have been banned by the American FDA from use in food production since 1984 and in food-producing animals since 1991; the same are also banned for shrimp culture even in India. Their continuance and detection forced a number of Indian firms to be listed for Detention without Physical Examination (or "Red List") under the import alerts. These rejections happened despite the existing inspection procedures prevalent in the country pertaining to the export of marine products. The Coastal Aquaculture Authority, Marine Products Export Development Authority (MPEDA) and Export Inspection Council are the key bodies in the country to monitor the use of antibiotics in shrimp farming as well as shrimp products prior to export.

The experts indicate that there is a dearth of high-end instrumentation uniformly across the country, which can detect antibiotic residues at lower limits of their concentration. The CSE has highlighted the need to pay more attention to government bodies, policymakers and stakeholders for addressing multiple issues. These are unregulated antibiotic availability, farmer and consumer awareness, biosecurity, monitoring and capability building and improving veterinary oversight for a greater outreach.[10]

The FDA rejects more snacks from India than any other country. According to its website, Indian products were found to contain high levels of pesticides, mould and the bacteria salmonella, a report in the *Wall Street Journal* (WSJ) said. The report mentions that more than half of all snacks that were tested and then restricted from being sold in the US this year were from India, which also leads the number of snack rejects across the world.[11]

"Key issue was India's inability to fully comply with international norms, such as the Codex Alimentarius".[12]

> "*There is a variance in food standards, resulting in persistent import refusals by regulators such as the FDA. This is a concern and companies need to look at this closely," said Ashwin Badri, chief executive officer of Equinox Labs, a Mumbai-based laboratory specialising in food, water and air testing.*[13]

The Minister of State for Commerce and Industry Nirmala Sitharaman said in a written reply to the Rajya Sabha that "the US health regulator has refused entry of 11,664 Indian products, including drugs, into the American market between January 2011 and February 2016.

> *"According to refusal report data available on the US Food and Drug Administration (USFDA) website, 11,664 refusals of Indian products were recorded from January 2011 to February 2016."*[14]

The products from India that were denied entry into the US included medicine, bakery products, fried snacks, spices, basmati rice, fisheries and herbals, she added. Dietary supplements, hair dyes and colours were also part of the no-entry list. "The reason given for the refusal varies from problems in branding to packaging, labelling and adulteration," the minister said.

Elaborating on the steps taken by the government to improve standards and quality to international levels, the minister said: "The steps taken by the government include tightening labelling rules and making it mandatory for companies to clearly mention the dates of manufacturing." Other steps include improving pre-export inspection, greater emphasis on standards through sensitisation of exporters for compliance of regulatory issues through export promotion agencies and also taking up the issue at bilateral trade forums wherever possible, Sitharaman said.[15]

Such negative reports put strong doubts on Indian production, manufacturing and exporters and ultimately on "Brand India". Imagine the level of confidence of the American companies or American markets on the Indian-imported goods in America, when they know that rejections are the highest for Indian products, that too when we don't have more than 2 per cent of overall American Imports? Comparing this with China, Canada, Mexico, Germany, Japan and other exporters, etc. we are too complacent and take quality control and auditing for granted.

The growth of Indian exports suffers due to large number of rejections; which are for the following reasons poor quality, non-compliance to their American standards, adulteration, residue traces and presence of pollutants, wrong packing or labelling, non-disclosure of required information, wrong production practices, violation of labour laws, human rights, unethical treatment of animals, etc. All such rejections can be easily avoided if the exporters are made aware of such issues on time.

The Export Inspection Council (EIC) presently has around 38 such labs which issue certification to exporters and are the premier agency for India. How can a country as large as India be reliant on just 38 labs to check and certify the quality of products being exported? This is a reflection of our seriousness, our lack of commitment and awareness to quality. This is the typical Indian *"Chalta Hai"* attitude; unfortunately this attitude is not going to help us achieve our goals.

Quality is a matter of strict compliance to procurement, production, post-production processes as well as labelling, packing and marketing. A vast majority of exporters, artisans, manufacturers, etc. don't have in house facilities to undertake any quality checks. So much so, that they may not be aware about the American or other International standards or phytosanitary compliance requirements or to the basic fact that environmental pollution is a major concern for their prospective buyers and that they must refrain from using chemicals, processes, etc. which are not acceptable to the American markets. There is an urgent need to look into manufacturing and supply side constraints that the exporters face. The large export houses and manufacturers may have some mechanism, tools and trained personnel to check quality, but the small exporters or new exporters lack such facilities or control on quality, resulting in exports of sub-standard products/services. Their rejections reflect poorly on India and build a very negative perception about Indian products and services.

While the Food Safety and Standards Authority of India (FSSAI) has attempted to bring some parity with international norms by introducing an ingredient-based regulatory regime in place of a product-based approval system, there is still much work to be done.[16]

A concentrated attempt is required to bring the Indian standards closer to the international standards, and the listing of standards, certification of products, etc. all shall be such that a cross-referencing of it is possible. The Indian trade bodies, Indian Standards Institute, and EIC labs can help by listing the applicable standards and other statutory compliances that are required. The same can be prominently displayed on the website or trade portals as well as at the labs. The exporters would have an easy access and they can themselves check. Chinese manufacturers and exporters display such certifications (product complying with American, European, ISO or Japanese standards) very prominently on their products, and use them smartly as a marketing tool as well as a differentiator from their competitors.

One of the other challenges while setting out standards in India is that they are mostly in the English language, which is not the language of the workforce in the food and agriculture sector. Many of the prohibitions, sampling and quality check processes get lost on the farmers, who have almost a nil understanding of English. It is very important for the Indian government to translate these standards in their regional languages so that they understand. However, the best would be to conduct training camps at farms and at agriculture institutes so that they get practical knowledge on the dos and don'ts.

The need for labs and the role they play is to be fully understood, i.e. they not only help in maintaining quality but also in R&D, introducing new processes, new technologies, new materials, innovations and increasing productivity. They need to be an integral part of any infrastructure that the government plans in the future for a manufacturing or exports cluster.

Apart from the labs helping in maintaining the quality, they also second as an audit agency to monitor and suggest improvements and for pointing out deficiencies in the infrastructure, processes and environment and health and safety compliances. The United States has opened up its base (FDA labs) in India to check the quality standards of the pharmaceuticals being manufactured in India. India should have more US-approved laboratories and auditing firms to comply with American standards. This will encourage Americans to trust more Indian products.

The government can create a positive push and acceptance of Indian products in the international markets by pushing further the Export Inspection Council (EIC), setting up a minimum of 5,000 certified laboratories and auditing and monitoring services to undertake quality certification, process compliance certification and compliance to sanitary and phytosanitary conditions. The first 500 such labs need to be urgently set up within two years, another 1,000 in the next two years and 3,500 in the final two years' time frame.

The Indian government can work along with the American government on creating guidelines and certification process for the new labs. This presents an opportunity to the American companies to also set up their labs here. The government can give license to private domestic and international players in the industry to start these lab chains. Each of the labs must go through a stringent checking process by the Indian government and then certified. These chains not only will help in Indian products getting acceptance in the American market, but worldwide. This would also force and help the Indian industry to bring in technological changes, instrumentation and skill set, thereby upgrading the entire manufacturing process in India and bringing about a quality change in the domestic market also.

Quality management is not just about adhering to quality standards once, but doing it each and every time a product is manufactured for shipment. This has to get into the DNA of every Indian manufacturer and service provider and every Indian exporter, and laboratories are the essential tool for imbibing that culture in our manufacturing and exports.

5. Design Banks: Design as a Differentiator

> *Design is everything, because without it we have no business. Anybody can design a decent product. They can't all design outstanding products. So, design is the differentiator...CEO Pentland Brands plc. (owners of Speedo).*

These words from the CEO of Pentland Brands, which owns the world-famous brand Speedo in swimming gear, captures the importance of "design".

What is Design? People often confuse aesthetics with design and also consider design as important for only expensive or sophisticated products. It is associated wrongly only with products, whereas in reality is it plays a very critical role in every aspect of the business that is conducted nowadays. Service design is as important as product design. The design scope is way beyond aesthetics (as aesthetics is only related to external look and feel); it encompasses an entire system of production and its life cycle. Design is multidimensional and is the bridge between an idea, a concept and the final product/service, to marketing and servicing to the end of its life.

> *Design is the driving force of the entire manufacturing process. We no longer just design components and products that are easy to manufacture and assemble. Instead, design these days considers the entire life cycle, from concept to manufacture, to maintenance and repair, right through to end of life processing. Dick Elsy, CEO, High Value Manufacturing Catapult.*[17]

As Bill Buxton, chief scientist of Microsoft, reminds us, products are the individual, social and cultural experiences that they engender and the value and impact that they have on others Hence design is about the experience of a product, system or service. Design is an interdisciplinary interpretive force that is able to analyse inventions to suggest paths for actual products and services that either meet or create consumer demand, bridging between raw invention and application. Design knowledge matches human capacities and needs, in all their variability and complexity, with technologies, leading to the creation of new value-added products.[18]

India ranks abysmally at 43rd out of 45 countries in a global innovation index, according to a report released by the US Chambers of Commerce.[19] In another report published in *Business Standard*, India has improved its innovation ranking in GII to reach 66th position from its last year's rank of 81st; this improvement in the rank for India comes after five years of a continuous drop in its ranking.[20] Any which way we look upon India's ranking, it is dismal and at the bottom of the innovation pyramid. This poor record has its roots lying in India's reluctance to acknowledge design as a key component of innovation. There is a famous saying in India, "Why to re-invent the wheel, simply look around and copy the wheel". We need to bring this attitude change towards design; we need to question the Wheel itself and find out for ourselves and focus on re-inventing it. By including design as part of the innovation paradigm (research and development and design) we could transform India's lackluster innovation record.

Design, today has become integral to innovation, production of goods and services that meet regulatory requirements; it has become more experiential enhancing the user experience. It has become the differentiator. Design has become vital for the exports to grow. A research undertaken by the Design Council of UK, demonstrated that for every £1 that companies invest in design to support their growth, they can expect to have a return of £5 in exports.[21]

Design can help manufacturers and service providers who wish to export to America by helping them to understand the American consumers and their requirements, existing products, gaps and the opportunities that the new Indian products or services can fulfil. Design can help Indian exporters to overcome competition, bring down the barriers and present new opportunities. Design can help the Indian product services to adapt and innovate to American requirements and comply with local standards and other environmental considerations. Design can enhance communication and marketing, labelling, packaging, branding, etc. which are all integral parts of the export cycle. Design is not only critical for high-end products and services, it is equally important for lower-end products. Design has as much a role to play in agriculture and food processing as much as in software development. Design plays a role of enabler for sectors like handicrafts, handloom, jewellery, footwear design, etc. Design multiplies the value system and works best when it is an integral part of the manufacturer or exporter's organisational culture and values. It is applicable to all manufacturing and service providers, be they individuals, SMEs or large corporate houses. It is relevant from heavy engineering-based products to products crafted by hands.

Indian artisans are fabulous and their expertise is unmatched; however for exports, Indian handicrafts come out too expensive as the artisan has to spend too much of time on producing the masterpiece. The buyers place orders for bulk quantities; the Indian artisans are not equipped to handle such orders, hence they either let these opportunities slip by or if they do take up the order, falter while producing them and end up making losses due to a high rejection rate. Unfortunately, such masterpieces act as prototypes and the real benefits are taken by mass producers in China for such handicraft. Design can be a tool here for such artisans, as design is not the final outcome, but the entire process. If each step of the process is well designed and recorded, it leads to step-by-step standardisation; it becomes easier for the artisan to reproduce his/her creation. It helps in scaling up the production, it helps in increasing productivity, capacity, wastage minimisation, time management, process management, quality management, helping him/her being right...every time. Design helps in bringing cost efficiencies and ownership of intellectual property, which till date has been an alien concept for the Indian artisans. Design improves profitability.

The growth of sectors like handloom, handicrafts, footwear, apparels, jewellery, etc. is also dependent on designs. The trends change, and these artisans and workers being traditional in their approach and production processes may not have access to new trends and even if they do, they need support in terms of understanding the production process. Currently, either the artisans continue to follow their own traditional products or they will match the design provided by the exporter, which the exporter too may have got from the client. The process becomes more of a sweat shop outsourcing, and the real value is lost.

Indian artisans and exporters will be able to generate more revenue and competitiveness if they are able to attain a leadership position in design too. However the challenge is of establishing an in-house design studio, as they will be too expensive unless a scale in exports or production is achieved. The Government of India can help by setting up design banks in exports clusters or manufacturing hubs. This will provide easy access to exporters and manufacturers for the latest trends and products that are in vogue in the US and other international markets. The understanding of US trends and their preferences is vital if exports to America are to be encouraged. Their choices, their living standards, culture and sensitivities are way different from other developed nations. To understand that because a product is successful in the EU or Japan or even in neighbouring Canada would automatically mean that it would be acceptable and successful in the US would be a grave mistake. So 'one size fits all' approach would not work.

The Indian software industry has developed leaps and bounds in the last three decades, and today India has the capability to research and design new software, new apps, new digital solutions. The IT industry has been the industrial revolution for India, it has catapulted India into a new league. However,Indian companies are still focussing on the lower-end of the value chain, especially for exports. They need to leap forward, and Research & Design can provide those wings. Data mining can help identify new angles, new access, and new opportunities to Indian IT firms. Thankfully, designing in the digital world is not as cumbersome, time-taking and expensive an exercise as it is for manufacturing. The opportunity for Indian IT in the other service sectors is wide open; all it needs is a little push and confidence. Service sectors like healthcare and wellness monitoring, transportation, tourism, entertainment, education, law, engineering, architecture and interior design, omni-channel retailing, banking and financial services are wide open for the IT to innovate and grow in. Concepts like virtual reality, proofing, testing and analytic modelling are yet to be explored to their full potential.

India needs another movement like "Make in India" and "Digital India" to help create and establish Design Banks & Research Institutes (DBRI). It is a novel concept whose time has come. The government can push various trade bodies and associations to create these design banks and research institutes. Like the CSR cess which has been made compulsory for the corporates to support social and economic upliftment of the Indian society, an equivalent emphasis has to be there for promoting a culture of innovation. Indian companies should willingly embrace the initiative and can commit 1 to 2 per cent of their profits as their contribution for setting these design banks. The Indian government can create an operating framework for the same and let the trade bodies, manufacturers and exporters benefit from it.

A design bank shall have in-house or outsourced designers, who may be experts in their field and are trained design professionals or product designers and engineers. They may develop their own designs and the same can be provided to the exporters at a fee. The designer would be completely responsible for detailing out the design and for certifying the product. The design banks can be an integral part of all engineering, medical, architectural, professional institutes or trade colleges. Not only would it help in providing hands-on-training to the students but also help them contribute through research, innovations and new ideas. The Institutes can undertake live problems on hand and suggest solutions. The exporter/manufacturer/artisan may also seek help on a project basis from the design bank and the experts may work on the assigned project for a fee or royalty. The designers may create a portfolio and share through the bank.

Product designing and engineering are crucial to introducing a new line of products and improvise on existing products. This is based on a lot of research and access to design tools. The local artisans or workers will gain from the same. The Indian frugal engineering attitude would help bring the costs down and can also help in improvising the production processes. We must leverage it. India's Mars mission and various satellite missions are shining examples of Indian frugal engineering, overcoming all kinds of obstructions, sanctions and technical challenges. The Indian Mars mission was the cheapest-ever mission by any nation, and that too, accomplished in its first attempt. If Indian scientists and engineers could achieve that, then there is no reason to doubt their capabilities to provide frugal design solutions to new machines and equipments required by the Indian crafts people and industrialists.

Online research collaboration between various research companies in India and America shall be encouraged. Contractual research, data collection, testing and designing shall help India understand new technological and design breakthroughs. Service design shall be able to match the future trends and challenges. The way products and services function today is not how they will operate tomorrow. Digital technology, 3D printing, nanotechnology, carbon fibres, silicon, optical fibres and online communication are going to change products and services and newer demands will arise with changing human behaviour. The start of this change, this new demand, would be from developed nations like America, so it would be in India's interest today to be future-ready and establish Design & Research institutes today so that they are able to be relevant to exports.

To be relevant to the American markets, the Indian exporters and service providers must adapt Indian ideas to American dreams. Similarly in India, American ideas need to be streamlined with Indian realities and expectations. Design banks and Research Institutes would play an important part in it.

6. Training, Training, Training...the Mantra for Success

The mantra to maintain timely quality deliverables is training, as it helps being right every time. It helps inculcating an organisational culture and commitment towards quality, maintaining productivity and profitability.

The American market is a very developed and sophisticated market; the quality of products and services is quite high. The national industrial standards in the US, both for providing services and goods, are different from other countries and compliance to them is mandatory for a product or service to be successful. Any shortcoming is an invitation to legal hassles and financial damages. Their lifestyle, habits and expectations are very different from us Indians. The working culture and sensitivity levels are different towards time, money, work-culture and environment. To be successful once is easy, but to remain successful for a long time requires a lot of hard work, refinement of processes and ensuring a quality output. All this can be achieved only through training...continuous upgradation both in knowledge and practice. Unfortunately, training is seen as a cost in India and not as an investment. We start profiling ourselves and our co-workers into a certain role and are happy sticking to it for years. The pace of change is very fast, new technologies and newer software are easing out many manufacturing issues, and still they are constantly being challenged by newer issues. The face of change is more sophistication, more digitalisation and being more tech-savvy, and this is where India faces a challenge. It has a "*Chalta hai*" (anything goes) attitude towards upgradation and training.

This attitude is like a death-knoll on the issue of trade...

The attitude of "this is India and things happens like this only in India".... The attitude like we know everything and the world shall accept the way we operate is not going to do any favour to India. We have a false superiority complex about ourselves; we take pride in our mythological history and claim that we know it all. Unfortunately this false pride is so imbibed in our system, that our approach towards formal education, training and practice has been badly mutilated, adding misery to all this is our ongoing flirtation with the age-old caste system and religious profiling. There are certain jobs in manufacturing or manufacturing sectors which till date are felt fit for 'lower caste' resources, and since it is for them and they have been doing it for ages, so there is no need to change, as we feel that they are happy about it and there is no need to spend any money on it.

An example of this could be the leather and footwear sector, where till date skinning, cleaning and preparation of hide/leather, tanning etc., are still undertaken by people of certain castes. They are economically poor, illiterate or poorly educated and socially oppressed, hence their exposure to new technologies, new processes, awareness about health and safety issues, understanding of environmental impact, etc. are too low. Very little attempt is made on ground to understand and make change in their lives and their working environment. To increase India's exports in the leather and footwear sector, it is very important to embrace them equally and train them on modern tools, equipment and processes and provide them with an opportunity to rise up and participate in product development and bringing in innovations that can take the sector way ahead in the competition. Another similar example is of meat exports which has been held hostage for long due to a heavy mix of religion and politics.

The aquaculture and food processing sectors have long suffered due to the inept handling of produce during the pre-harvesting and post-harvesting processes. It is estimated that around 25–30 per cent of the produce is lost in-between due to inept handling of the fruits and vegetables. The farmers or the producers do not provide much training as being seasonal, most of the pre-harvesting processes are handled by migrant labourers. Sorting, packing, loading and unloading are all done through outdated modes, resulting in further losses. All this could be easily avoided by adopting proper training workshops and training workers. It would have helped in stemming the rot and help the sector become more productive and competitive. There is an acute shortage of professionals with an expertise in packing. The Indian Institute of Packaging with its head office situated at Mumbai and its branches located at Delhi, Kolkata, Chennai, Hyderabad, Bengaluru and Guwahati, provide short-term and long-term courses. Such branches should be opened in all the states as they not only support exports, but also help in the domestic market. The government can permit the international institutes to set up training campuses and offer such courses in India.

TQM (Total Quality Management), TPM (Total Productivity Management), ISO (International Organisation for Standardisation), BS (British Standards) and JIT (Just in Time)are the common buzzwords, which if the Indian workers could understand and inculcate, would do a great good to Indian manufacturing and exports. However, currently these are being seen from the prism of management and not as productivity tools. This attitude can be changed by thorough training.

Over-reliance on the boss, and the attitude that the boss is always right, has roots in some ground reality, because India lacks talent in the exports industry. Usually, because of the learning on the job and being small, dependence onboss is much more as all the decision-making rests with the boss, who has a habit of being involved in every aspect of the business – from interacting with the customer and dealing with suppliers, to being a marketer and the chief quality controller. The boss is the omnipresent God in his fiefdom. Sadly, that is not going to help the Indian exports.

To avoid such scenarios, the government must push for setting up professional courses, training programmes for opening professional colleges, and training centres for each of the product category, for workers, mid-management level and ancillary services.

Most of the current professional courses in exports are oriented towards marketing, trade documentation and custom clearances, and this, too, in the metros. What India needs is an all-round training at every level of the trade process, and such training institutes should be promoted to be set-up in all export clusters, with customised courses for each cluster requirement.

Currently, there is a huge shortfall of right resources at each process of export across each of the product categories.

- Production processes: from raw to finished goods
- Technology and tools
- Quality and production management
- Product handling at various stages of its production life cycle
- Introduction to international standards, sanitary and phytosanitary compliance requirements and other compliances.
- Research & Development: state-of-the-art equipped labs, frugal engineering, product design and engineering, introduction to IPR and patents, safeguarding trade secrets, etc., International Market Research, testing and expansion
- International marketing and international trade
- Packaging, labelling and storing
- Trade logistics management
- Foreign languages
- International trade laws, treaties and agreements and trade negotiations

The Indian government must invite American experts and train the workforce here in its respective fields of operation. Workshops, seminars and other engagement platforms must be arranged for the lower and mid-level employees to understand new technologies and processes. Hands-on-experience shall be given prominence in training. The government must work on schemes and initiatives to help exporters and manufacturers to constantly train their employees, providing them with international exposure and working on training labs set with modern machines and equipment. Genuine certification for training must be ensured, so that it is valued and rewarded. The government can put new initiatives like scholarships for training or interest-free training loans to the manufacturer or exporter. The role of Indian trade bodies, manufacturing and service provider associations and exporter associations is significant and vital to formulate the gap and the training modules required. Sector experts must be engaged to formulate the curricula for various training programmes and their durations. Evening and night time training labs/studios shall be promoted aggressively, so that working employees have access to better training facilities.

To ensure that the manufacturers and exporters gain from the investments that they have made in upgrading the skill-set of their workers/ employees, the government should promote change in labour laws so that an employee is committed to the manufacturer or employer for a certain period of time, and unless he/she gets a no-objection certificate for this period successfully being completed, no other employer shall hire him/ her. There should be provision of recovering the costs from a rogue employee for deliberate violations. Similarly, the rights of employees need to be safeguarded.

One of the key challenges faced often by the exporters is the lack of understanding of foreign languages. Although Indians have a fair share of English speaking/understanding population, yet when it comes to trade laws and other contractual documentation, the barrier of language becomes evident. This is more pronounced and visible for other foreign languages like French, Spanish, Italian, Chinese, Japanese, Russian, German and Arabic, etc. French and Spanish languages are important because they are the two languages (after English) that are spoken and understood in many of the nations across the world. India must promote these languages and they must be taught in institutes and schools, especially in those providing courses in international marketing.

7. Financial Assistance

Most of the manufacturers, especially the small and medium-sized enterprises (SMEs) and service providers, are reluctant to export to foreign markets. They remain content to cater to the domestic markets. Unfortunately, access to capital remains a sizable obstacle for the SMEs looking to become exporters. Exports is usually a more expensive exercise than dealing with the domestic markets as export activities create a number of capital demands, right up-front, beyond those involved in the domestic market: international marketing and sales, distribution network, order fulfilment, shipping and trade compliance that often involve much greater investments of time and money than does domestic trade. This is the reason why 90 per cent of international trade is dependent upon export finance and export insurance by banks or financial institutions.[22] According to Auboin (2009), ninety per cent of international trade involves trade finance.[23] This also explains the reason why export incentives are widely employed as a strategy of export promotion. The main aim of these incentives is to increase the profitability of export business (though artificially). The important export incentives in India include the rebate on duties, cash compensatory support, income tax concession, interest subsidies, freight subsidy, etc.

Given these various costs, the access to capital is of critical importance to most companies looking to grow through exporting. The SMEs face particular challenges in accessing capital, given their smaller size, limited assets, and general inability to raise funds through credit markets or publicly traded equity. Given that the SMEs tend to have greater volatility in earnings and growth than large companies, they are often seen as riskier investments by the banks and other financial institutions and hence they are charged a higher rate of interest.

Furthermore, the assessment of credit worthiness, asset valuation, financial history and other kinds of paperwork take too much of time sometime to the point that the new entrepreneur or new exporter is discouraged to export. Already overloaded with non-performing assets, banks too are wary of financing exports and even less inclined to work with SMEs. These challenges are compounded by the risk involved in an alien country, especially for customers demanding longer credit periods (some asking beyond 120–180 days), exchange rate instability and the worst, cases of customer non-payment.

The Indian government is well aware of these issues as they are continuously being raised by the export trade bodies and associations. The Indian government has taken many steps to encourage banks to lend to SMEs and push the growth of exports through manufacturing and services. The government has been nudging the banks to reduce the interest rates to the SMEs; they may still be reluctant to issue loans for small export-related transactions, given their diminished appetite for small business loans and their exposure to the non-guaranteed portion of the loan.

The government has been trying through various types of export schemes and incentives to attract manufacturers and service providers to exports. The government has been rolling out doles to push exports. This approach has lived its life and is not going to be fruitful anymore. Also, with the proposed GST soon going to become a reality, the manufacturers and exporters would be far more hit and discouraged from exporting, as this cost competitiveness is going to be badly affected and also there is not going to be too much of cost variation between the domestic and international market. They would then be more inclined to cater to the domestic market than to export.

India itself being a large market, thankfully, provides a domestic market to manufacturers and traders to safeguard any excess capacity created, and since the gap is currently quite large, there is no pitfall for the government if it looks into providing a well-directed and cheap finance available to the manufacturing and exports sector. Instead of subsidies, incentives, etc., it would be best if a mechanism of providing long-term preferential loans to the exporters, or to intermediate service providers to set up infrastructure that supports manufacturing and trade is provided.

The existing approach of incentives to promote exports needs to be redefined and a course correction needs to be undertaken. Many of the incentives provided by the government work at cross-purposes with each other and harm the long-term exports agenda as well keeping it alive, supported through expensive life support means (read artificially supported). Incentives should be directed towards improving quality, compliances, time efficiency and not just towards the quantity or value of imports or exports for profitability. With the GST being rolled out in the near future, the current incentives may have to be either abolished or modified. Many of the incentives are not in compliance with WTO guidelines and framework; they need to be relooked into. In the changing scenario in the world, it is best to go by the rule book of the WTO while looking into providing incentives, which may be punished by the importing country by levying new taxes or charges. This would be counterproductive and Indian exports can ill-afford that.

For example:

> *For the food processing industry and exports, one of the most important infrastructure requirements is the cold storage facilities. There is an acute shortage of cold storage facilities in India; hence, instead of providing incentives or subsidies to exporters for exporting a product which may be contrary to the WTO guidelines, it would be advisable to give financial assistance to set up a cold storage facility, which will not only help exporters but also the Indian market. The cost increase of the product while being processed due to loss in harvest in the absence of the cold storage facility is much higher than the incentive the exporter gets from the government. Not only the government would have provided the facility, it would have helped the producer/exporter to bring down the cost of the product and thus making it more competitive, without flouting any norms. This way not only precious produce can be saved, but also that the government help goes in the right direction. Instead of rewarding incompetence, the government is supporting and creating productive infrastructure.*

This can be done by further expanding and setting up additional special financial institutes and banks focused on exports and manufacturing on lines of the EXIM Bank. The government can invite investments into these banks by issuing bonds, or raising capital through equity market or all together permitting 100 per cent FDI in such financial institutes. It would be in India's interest to have a healthy competition amongst the financial institutes for promoting and supporting Indian exports.

These special export-oriented financial institutes shall help in the following objectives:

i) Export Expansion and Working Capital Financing

It must help the Indian exporters to obtain loans that facilitate the export of goods or services by providing the financial resources needed to propagate exports and compete more aggressively and efficiently in the international market.

- **Export-focused Small Business Working Capital Programme:** these banks can provide up to US$50,000 in short-term, transaction-specific working capital loans to small business exporters. The uses of this financing shall include pre-export financing of labour and materials and post-shipment financing of the accounts receivable generated from transaction-specific overseas sales.
- **Working Capital Guarantee Programme:** provides transaction-specific working capital loans to exporters, backed by a state government guarantee. The uses of this financing shall include: purchasing finished products for export; paying for raw materials, equipment, supplies, labour and overhead to produce goods and/or provide services for export; covering standby letters of credit serving as bid bonds, performance bonds, or payment guarantees and financing foreign receivables.
- **Export Scouting Programme:** provides small businesses that have exporting potential, but need funds to cover the initial costs of entering an export market, with up to US$50,000 in export development financing to produce goods or to provide services for export.

ii) Capacity Building Financing

This would help the Indian manufacturers, service providers and exporters to acquire, construct, renovate, modernise, improve or expand facilities and equipment to produce goods or services involved in international trade.

These banks or financial institutions would be responsible for tracking investments, assets, trade funding, insurances and payment gateways for international financial dealings. Their approach will be more professional and well directed, when the experts in the sector evaluate and approve the loan requirements and monitor the market and progress made by the exporter. Hence, the possibility of bad assets being created and the Indian government being saddled with them would be minimal. Like any open market, the interest rates will be dependent upon market dynamics.

The Indian government can also permit states to customise export finance support for the particular needs of their respective industries. By stepping up the strengthening of SME exporters' access to capital, each state can tailor its interventions to best suit its SME and lender base and export objectives. The states can be permitted to raise bonds and other such financial instruments to help the SMEs with their export-oriented capacity expansion plan; the state can stand guarantee for SME loans for capacity expansion for exports for two years to five years depending upon its own assessment.

The credit period for pre-shipment and post-shipment shall be increased as the buyers in international markets are demanding higher credit periods to make payments. The government shall consider doubling the credit period as it will give a major elbow room to exporters. However, this should be insured to protect the banks.

The financial institutes like EXIM can help specially in exports of services from India. The risks involved are less and the impact on creating quality and price differential are more and favourable for the Indian service exporters.

In the current situation, when international trade has to scale protectionism and economic slowdown in countries where India exports majorly, one possible way to push the export growth is to snatch the market share from other competing countries, through competitive pricing, which can be achieved by cutting down the borrowing cost on export credit.

If any incentives are to be provided then the same shall be directed towards the NE states and other states which are deficient in basic infrastructure and need government support through incentives for exports.

8. Grading

The mechanism to put fraudulent, cheating and unprofessional exporters, who dupe many of the foreign clients and spoil India's reputation, must be put into place. Similarly, Indian importers must share their experience to ensure that the Indian traders and companies are not cheated by overseas companies and traders.

Export houses, trading houses, 'Star' trading houses and 'Superstar' trading houses are a categorisation currently being used by the Indian government to incentivise the exporters through various schemes. The objective of the scheme is to recognise established exporters with a view to building marketing infrastructure and expertise required for export promotion. The eligibility criterion for such recognition is currently on the basis of the FOB/NFE value of export of goods and services, including software exports made directly, as well as on the basis of services rendered by the service provider during the preceding three licensing years or the preceding licensing year, at the option of the exporter. The exports made both in free foreign exchange and in Indian Rupees, are taken into account for the purpose of recognition...[24]

The central idea behind the above-mentioned categorisation is to provide incentives for the export target achieved. However, it does little in stating the quality of the exports or the deliverable timelines and client relationship. It is also silent on the exporters' relationship with their suppliers and their compliance status to Indian and international markets. The same can be done easily by implementing and undertaking a new Grading & Certification of Indian Exporters, or make relevant additions and modifications to protect the interest of international clients and to safeguard the Indian brands against adulterators, manipulators, thugs and repeat offenders. Each of the exporters must exhibit the grade while dealing with an international client. This will establish credibility amongst the world trading community. The government must link incentives and access to government facilities directly with the grading mechanism.

The grading mechanism shall be updated and reviewed every financial year and any change must reflect online as well as on the exporter's correspondence. The grading mechanism must also help the exporters have easy access to capital from financial institutes and other lenders.

A similar mechanism can be put in for exporters and importers where they can access and check the grading of the international buyer and sellers, before they get into a deal. This mechanism can help in ensuring and safeguarding the interests of the Indian traders, as well as act as motivation to move into the best possible grade, by improving upon various parameters set for grading.

The grading parameters could be:

- Financial rating, payment and credit history
- Quality satisfaction
- Quantity certifications
- Timeline commitments
- Packaging and branding compliances
- Environmental compliances
- Labour standard compliances
- Billing, documentation filing and compliances

9. Geographical Indication and Protection

Geographical Indication (GI) status is believed to be the oldest form of Intellectual Property (IP) protection.[25] The tag is given to authorised users in a certain country as a whole or in some part of the country, who can use it exclusively for the products produced, manufactured or crafted by the people in that region, and no unauthorised person is permitted to use the same.

GIs have been defined under Article 22(1) of the WTO Agreement on Trade-Related Aspects of Intellectual Property Rights (TRIPs) Agreement as: "Indications which identify a good as originating in the territory of a member – or a region or a locality in that territory – where a given quality, reputation or characteristic of the good is essentially attributable to its geographic origin".[26]

Geographical Indication helps the local community by giving recognition and protection on the markets to the names of these products. GI encourages investment by the community of producers in preserving the specific qualities of the product or a service on which the reputation is built. The GI tag provides a marketing tool and collective edge to the community and inspires it to invest and capitalise together in promoting and safeguarding the reputation of the product and the region. But there's no fool-proof method developed yet that ensures 100 per cent protection to a particular GI tag as the GI tag is for a product and not the actual knowledge associated with the product.

Supporters and campaigners of GI tags assert that the GI is a differentiator and a great marketing tool for the exporters, which can be used effectively to classify your produce and supplies at levels above your foreign competitors. "GI can be a valuable tool for export differentiation. As much as 85 per cent of French wine exports use GIs on their labels, as do 80 per cent of all spirits exported from EU. Geographical Indications have the potential to be India's growth engine".[27]

India currently has over 258 products tagged under GI,[28] and another 270 are in the process of being recorded and tagged. The number of GI's itself is proof enough of India's diversity, its rich traditional knowledge and craftsmanship. If we look closely into this list, we start to realise its relevance and impact on our heritage, art, culture, cuisine and local produce, which if marketed properly, can help the artisans, craftsmen, farmers, weavers, etc. to further develop and produce to help Indian exports. These GI-tagged products carry immense brand recognition and goodwill built over generations and have been traded for centuries. Indian handicraft products are being dubiously copied, counterfeited, mass produced and exported from the factories of China, under the guise of Indian handicrafts so much so that the Indians have started importing cheap imitations from China of the original Indian handicrafts.

It is for the protection of Indian handicrafts and the promotion of the original Indian products that it is important that the government steps in to make the GIs work well for Indian exports. An acute funds shortage amongst many registered GIs, lack of civil and criminal remedies in case of GI transgressions, absence of vigilant and regular inspections, reporting and recording of international violations and improper coordination between stakeholders involved in the value chain of exports of GI products, etc., are some areas that the government should look into.

Presently, the GI awareness campaigns by the government appear to be concentrated only on the registration of GI products. They need to come out with a strategic plan on promotion and branding. The government should involve the trade bodies and handicraft associations to carefully and scientifically list the unique properties of the GIs, so that the craftsmen, farmers and other stakeholders can be educated well to protect the GI tag. The trade bodies must also come up with concrete marketing and distribution plans and networks in both domestic and export markets.

As per a paper titled "Pre- and Post-Geographical Indications Registration Measures" by Kulkarni and Konde in the *Journal of Intellectual Property Rights*, "The Indian government has not made any headway in adopting strategies for branding and promotion of GI products or their marketing and distribution in both domestic and export markets." True that if industries like handicraft and others that create rural employment are to flourish, in the absence of massive pockets, the government has to take the GIs in all seriousness. "Make in India" is a good, steady development, but factories and warehouses will take their time to get established, and all of India is not skilled enough to be lifted from the farmlands and placed in factories.[29]

> *Dilip Kumar, director at Nazrana Chikan, has a similar story to tell. He says that GI registration is done in two parts – first the product and its area are registered, and then, the manufacturers and users of the product register themselves. Out of the thousands involved in Chikan work, he says woefully that only four have registered themselves. "There is no awareness of the product," he laments,*
>
> *"We need to popularise the art first within India, and then the world. If even 70 per cent people register themselves, the benefits will follow immediately."*[30]

The Indian government is sensitive to such malpractices and wrongful patents being awarded to foreign international firms; it needs to be further aggressive and alive to the GI-tagging issues. Few recommendations that may be helpful are as follows:

a) Funding for promotion and marketing through corporate sponsorship by permitting them under the CSR initiative;
b) Establishing a network of watchdogs to report and protect infringements of Indian GI. This could be through activists within the Indian diaspora or by hiring monitoring and auditing agencies worldwide. The initiative can be undertaken by involving Indian export and trade bodies, cooperatives, etc.;
c) Creating a consolidated data bank and design bank, through scientific research and involving experts, who can help record the entire process and uniqueness in details, and they can help the craftsmen to produce these products in large volumes for exports and with the same standardisation; and
d) The use of technology while labelling and branding. RFID tagging, Scanner codes, bar coding are few of the technologies which are easily available and shall be utilised to check on the origin of product, manufacturers' name, date, etc. This will help in detecting fake items. Holographic logos shall be used to certify the authenticity of the GI tagging.

The government shall promote the use of advanced systems like radio frequency identification (RFID) for GI products, for identification and tracking of an item through the whole supply chain globally. Every GI product item shall carry a permanently fixed RFID tag coded with information about the manufacturing source as well as the product specifications. The tag could be read by an RFID reader anywhere in the world and the information sent to a centralised station meant for validating the same. This way the government will not only be able to track and authenticate but also collect relevant data in terms of demand, duration of the demand as well as the time between the item being produced to being purchased. This helps them to anticipate and adjust the production accordingly. The follow-up after sales is as much important as is through the sales period. It would help to understand the gap in consumer expectations and if any modification or improvement needs to be done, the same can be guided through design banks to the local craftsmen, weavers and artisans.

Till now the government's focus has been on getting GI tagging for products; the same shall be tried for the service sector. There are many unique traditional practices such as the Kerala Massage, Naturopathy, Kalaripayattu, marmachikitsa, etc. which can garner additional exports revenue for India.

10. Marketing and Promotions

Various export promotion bodies (councils) have been set up by the Indian government to market and promote the Indian products and services. These bodies are quite active and have been trying to get the Indian exporters more exposure and encouraging them to be more aggressive in capturing a greater market share. There have been some rewards to these efforts being put in and the Indian exports have been growing worldwide. Nevertheless, the results are far from expectation and the growth pace has been much slower than anticipated. This means that the government and export promotion councils must have a relook at their approach and modify. Unless the export rate does not grow in leaps and bounds, India's share in the world export is going to be dismally low.

One of the reasons for the earlier recommendation of a "radical approach" is for the government to jump-start the exports marketing and promotions in America and other countries. Unless we have our experts in promotions embedded into the diplomatic missions and in trade bodies, it is going to be difficult to promote Indian exports correctly. The way technology and new strategies have changed every aspect of production, sales and service is also true for promotions.

Promotions have become more experiential and have moved away from the standard definitions of advertising and marketing. It is where people wish to engage, interact, feel, use and learn about themselves directly with the product or service. Social media platforms, E-commerce, digital marketing have brought in a major change on how the consumer interacts today. It is too diversified and India will have to reconsider its strategy on exports promotion.

Following are few of the recommendations that may sound similar to what the government is attempting; the difference is that a more structured approach is required. The engagement platforms will have to be more of Infotainment and more experiential.

a) Indian trade portals, websites of trade bodies, etc., are too generic and straight-jacketed. The information provided has to be more relevant and flexible.
b) Digital marketing and social media platforms shall be used to promote the Indian products in American and other international markets. Separate budgetary allocations shall be there for such campaigns.
c) The outdoor advertising medium is a very cost-efficient medium and has the flexibility of being customised to local requirements. Such mediums shall be used to market Indian goods and create awareness, and reassure about quality and service.
d) Radio is another medium, which has the flexibility of size and customisation to target the selected audience. Sponsorship, new radio programmes on awareness about India and its products shall be aired. It will help build a positive perception about India and Indian products and services. International celebrity endorsements as well as engaging Indian celebrities to promote India and Indian goods should be tried.
e) Establishing chain of experiential centres for encouraging locals to try out and experiment with Indian products, cuisines, handicrafts, consumer goods, etc. These centres can double up as market research as well as distribution points. The trade bodies can invest in these chains along with the local investors keen to partner them.
f) Hold India-centric events, fairs, trade meets, etc. and engage with all stakeholders (community-to-community engagement), entertainment, cultural programmes, exhibitions and DIY (do it yourself) camps, etc. Showcase India's achievements, contributions

and their commitment to the local community. This is required to offset any negative backlash, and to win hearts.

g) Sponsorship exchange programmes for training, education and research. Joint research programmes can also be initiated and sponsored by the Indian and foreign governments.

h) Create mega trade events in all parts of India to showcase and push exports. Such events shall be theme-based, mega in nature and longer in duration, well-integrated with discussion forums, training meets, buyer–seller meets, etc. Infrastructure for such events shall be in position, with convention centres, hotels, close proximity to the airports, etc.

i) Hold more training meets, buyer–seller meets, etc., in India to encourage domestic manufacturers and service providers to venture out in international markets.

j) International and national mentors and brand ambassadors shall be engaged and their services undertaken for promotions, as well as to provide insights, project trends and train Indian business houses.

k) Hire lobby groups and professional international exports promotion agencies to market and promote Indian products in new markets. This can be executed through trade bodies and councils.

l) Incentives for exposure to exporters, sponsoring workers, designers, engineers and technicians for international experience and participation in trade fairs and training meets, programmes for artisans and designers, etc.

END NOTES

1. https://www.census.gov/foreign-trade/statistics/state/data/index.html
2. https://www.census.gov/foreign-trade/statistics/state/data/index.html
3. http://www.chinausfocus.com/2022/wp-content/uploads/Part+02-Chapter+09.pdf
4. http://www.financialexpress.com/archive/gdp-loss-power-shortages-cost-india-68-bn-says-ficci/1175149/
5. http://ficci.in/Sedocument/20218/Power-Report2013.pdf
6. https://www.adb.org/sites/default/files/publication/177093/adbi-wp553.pdf
7. http://economictimes.indiatimes.com/news/economy/finance/india-incurs-21-3-billion-loss-due-to-delay-on-roads-study/articleshow/52639128.cms
8. http://timesofindia.indiatimes.com/india/13334-made-in-India-items-rejected-by-US-FDA-

in-6-yrs-1753-less-than-China/articleshow/50909128.cms
9. http://www.downtoearth.org.in/blog/fda-rejects-indian-shrimps-due-to-antibiotic-presence-54768
10. http://www.downtoearth.org.in/blog/fda-rejects-indian-shrimps-due-to-antibiotic-presence-54768
11. http://www.business-standard.com/article/companies/us-fda-rejects-more-snacks-from-india-than-any-other-country-115061100848_1.html
12. http://www.rediff.com/business/report/why-so-many-indian-food-product-exports-get-rejected/20160913.htm
13. http://www.rediff.com/business/report/why-so-many-indian-food-product-exports-get-rejected/20160913.htm
14. http://www.dnaindia.com/money/report-usfda-has-rejected-entry-of-11665-indian-products-into-america-since-jan-2011-sitharaman-2184774
15. http://www.dnaindia.com/money/report-usfda-has-rejected-entry-of-11665-indian-products-into-america-since-jan-2011-sitharaman-2184774
16. http://www.rediff.com/business/report/why-so-many-indian-food-product-exports-get-rejected/20160913.htm
17. http://futuresforumvgs.blogspot.in/2015/05/design-for-life-not-just-for.html
18. http://policyoptions.irpp.org/fr/magazines/innovation-nation/innovation-by-design-differentiator-in-the-digital-age/
19. http://www.hindustantimes.com/india-news/india-placed-at-43rd-among-45-nations-in-global-innovation-index/story-4gtIA7cWoUnaJklPe95BfJ.html
20. http://www.business-standard.com/article/news-cm/global-innovation-index-2016-india-improves-its-innovation-rank-15-positions-in-gii-2016-116082200336_1.html
21. http://www.designcouncil.org.uk/our-services/business-growth
22. http://www.nmims.edu/NMIMSmanagementreview/pdf/april-may-14/institutionalization-export-promotion-india-shivakumar-and-balbir.pdf
23. http://lare-efi.u-bordeaux4.fr/IMG/pdf/CR14-EFI03.pdf
24. http://pib.nic.in/archieve/eximpol/eximpol00-01/Chap-12.htm
25. https://www.thedollarbusiness.com/magazine/geographical-indication-tags—are-gi-tags-helping-india-s-exports-/45759
26. https://www.wto.org/english/docs_e/legal_e/27-trips_04b_e.htm
27. http://www.financialexpress.com/opinion/geographical-indications-have-the-potential-to-be-indias-growth-engine/234813/
28. https://en.wikipedia.org/wiki/List_of_Geographical_Indications_in_India
29. http://nopr.niscair.res.in/bitstream/123456789/13056/1/JIPR%2016%286%29%20463-469.pdf
30. https://www.thedollarbusiness.com/magazine/geographical-indication-tags—are-gi-tags-helping-india-s-exports-/45759

SECTION FOUR

MOVE THE NEEDLE

Indian Service Exports

In the coming future, the Indian service sector and its exports is going to be the key driver of Indian growth. Technology and Telecommunications have been a great leveller. Being less capital-intensive, more skill and knowledge-dependent and heavily in favour of human resource requirement, it provides India an edge in comparison to the production and manufacturing sector. If India wishes to be seated at the high table of global trade leaders, then the usual approach would not be in its favour. It would need fast pace decision-making, action and implementation across all levels of the government.

The US not only is India's biggest service import destination but can be a great enabler for India to achieve its goals. Correspondingly, India can value-add too many of the shortcomings that the US businesses face and provide them access to the world's biggest potential market. If the India–US trade relationship wishes to leap forward into the future, it will have to move the needle from "Dreaming to Doing".

The Economic Survey 2016–17, was tabled in the Parliament on January 31, 2017, by Mr. Arun Jaitley, Union Minister for Finance, Government of India. According to the economic survey of 2016–17 the services sector was projected to grow at 8.8 per cent in 2016–17, similar to 2015–16. As per the World Trade Organisation (WTO) data, India's commercial services exports increased from US$51.9 billion in 2005 to

US$ 155.3 billion in 2015, taking its share in the global services exports to 3.3 per cent in 2015 from 3.1 per cent in 2014.[1]

In terms of growth in the tourism sector, during January to December 2016, the Foreign Tourist Arrivals (FTAs) were 8.9 million with a growth of 10.7 per cent and the foreign exchange earnings (FEE) were at US$ 23.1 billion with a growth of 9.8 per cent.[2]

The focus of the current government shall aim to give Indian services the global visibility they rightly deserve. The services sector is hugely diverse and caters to a wide set of skill and technology levels; nevertheless, we feel that the focus sectors where India has great potential at the global level as well as with the US should be IT-BPM, healthcare, education, travel &tourism, logistics, aviation, media &entertainment, space, as well as the professional services of accounting &auditing, management consulting, architecture &engineering and legal services.

The US is already the number one importer of services from India, and with India's growing proficiency, favourable demographic profile, skill attainments and growing breed of entrepreneurs, the advantages are multiple for India – and it would do India great good if the policymakers can help further push it through positive comprehensive framework. The future is bright for India's service exports.

- It should aim for growing its share further within the US.
- Expand its exports to nations like Canada, UK, Australia, New Zealand and other nations where English is the language of the population.
- Firm up its position in the EU, Japan, Russia and other developed nations, where the potential is high, but language is a barrier. India will have to formulate a strategy on the same.
- India must create a strong first-mover advantage in the African continent, expand its footprint in the neighbourhood, i.e. in the Asian and West Asian countries.
- Reach out and explore aggressively the South American continent, which is a market which is still unexplored, but holds a good promise.

The Indian government has undertaken various initiatives to propel the growth of the Indian services sector with initiatives like the "Make in India" and "Digital India". These initiatives are gaining momentum and driving the expansion of services in the domestic space in India as well as internationally, especially in the United States of America. However, a lot more needs to be done to unravel the true potential of the Indian services sector, be it domestically or in the international market.

i) A lack of infrastructure is ailing the service exports as much it affects the manufacturing and goods exports. For instance, most IT companies have to invest in captive power units due to erratic power supply. This increases their costs and makes them non-competitive. Companies in the services sector like healthcare, tourism, logistic services, repairs and maintenance, educational institutes etc., find it difficult to acquire property due to the lack of urban planning, restrictive zoning regulations, outdated laws related to land conversion, lack of clear ownership and title of land, among others. This causes delays in project implementation. In addition, due to poor infrastructural planning, the full benefits of the existing investment cannot be reaped.

ii) A clear long-term vision for each of the key service sector is required. In the post-liberalisation period, the services sector has largely been left to grow on its own. There is no nodal ministry at the Centre for service sectors except where the government is responsible to provide services to the citizens like transport and power; there too the focus is much more on domestic compulsions rather than on service exports. Many services are under the purview of state governments or are jointly regulated by the central and state governments. The multiplicity of regulatory bodies creates a multiplicity of regulations and multiple clearance requirements.

iii) The foundation of any policy framework is credible data and research. A lack of empirical research in the area of services export remains the biggest hurdle along with a lack of reliable, timely and easily interpretable data. The data that is more widely available does not currently encompass all forms of trade in services. Moreover, there is a lack of distinction in the data collection procedure between goods and services within each sub-sector such as telecommunications and IT. What is required is the trade data on services at a more disaggregated level which is consistent with the value-added and employment data and is comparable across time. The data should be collected on a yearly basis for understanding the trends and there should be a centralised system of data collection and collation.

iv) Based on the research and data available, the government of India must formulate an Index of Services, in line with international practice, in order to have a coherent policy on services. Given the heterogeneity of services, the formulation of separate indices can also be considered. Also, the services sub-sector definitions in India do not match with international definitions which make it difficult to do cross-country analysis. There is an urgent need to have a clear definition of sub-sectors, based on international definitions like the UNCPC.

v) Since the services sector is heterogeneous, it is important to identify the most important trade barriers faced by the different services sub-sectors and then undertake sector-specific reforms.

vi) A blueprint to accomplish the goals for each service sector listed in the service index, a shared vision of all stakeholders and the expansion of an ever-evolving environment is required.

vii) Accountability and responsibility alignment amongst stakeholders and a monitoring mechanism with reality checks need to be in place.

viii) Since the US, the UK and theEU at present constitute the majority share in service exports from India, the policy framework must stress upon the quality of services as well as their compliance to the international standards and laws.

ix) A majority of the services are exported from tier-2, tier-3 cities in different states, and there are disparities in performance across states and the poor states seem to do badly in services infrastructure and in its delivery. The policies have to focus on state-wise requirements.

x) A holistic and more practical view should be aligned towards regulatory reforms and must follow international best practices; currently, some regulations do not take into account technological developments while others are completely outdated or do not often follow the international best practices. There is a lack of prescribed standards and a common accreditation process. Need is warranted to build confidence of the international community towards the services being provided from India; accreditation will help in process compliances, labour law compliances, quality assurances as well as environmental, health and safety norm compliances.

The policy framework has to be sympathetic to a new breed of entrepreneurs, who should be encouraged to innovate and offer new solutions in their respective service sectors. The focus on SMEs in the service exports is essential and critical as they form the backbone of many service sectors such as tourism, professional services and logistics.

The same is essential to move away from the lower end of the value chain to the upper end. It is also required to change the perception of India as a sweat shop of the West. We need to come out of the H1B visa blackmail and look beyond the BPO sector. India has the strength, potential and opportunities a plenty; we just need to be imaginative, have faith, plan well and fight on our strengths. It is not to say that we don't have issues – we do have plenty of them. The only possibility is the way ahead; removing each one of them at a faster pace. The biggest disservice that a government can do to India, is to give a false sense of security and hold it on artificial support mechanism of financial doles; instead, it needs to work with stakeholders and come up with a policy framework, which supports the creation of infrastructure, resource base, research and innovation and the appetite to take on bigger and bigger challenges.

India has great many vacuums that need to be filled in; India has challenges in infrastructure, research and technology, and Americans can contribute towards the same, and in the process, benefit and come closer to the goals set in by Trump's administration. There are numerous opportunities for both the nations to work together and fulfil the vision they hold. India and the US are to be viewed as complimentary to each other at all levels of the services sector, and they can achieve the same provided they are both open-minded and flexible to the challenges they face. Being selfish, obstructionist and protectionist is nothing short of hara-kiri in today's reality. Both America as well as India will have to give space to each other; a rigid approach won't yield any substantial result. It can be easily assumed that both Trump and Modi are going to be in the driving seat for long, and being stubborn and confrontationist is not in the interest of the American or the Indian citizens.

The service industry being relatively new has an advantage of being more organised than manufacturing, making it easier to be regulated and monitored. The issues like IP infringement, patents, data theft and security etc., are easier to legislate and be addressed.

The biggest difference between the services and produced goods is that while a produced or manufactured good can be stored for later consumption by its consumer, the service gets consumed while getting produced. In that sense, the service has an advantage as well as disadvantage of time. Unless the quality of service is not good or consistent with the benchmark of time, there are little chances of it surviving for long. Hence, the understanding of time and necessity to take the right decision at the right time is much more urgent for this sector. A service can be totally out of business in a short time, unless it has the flexibility to adapt and bounce back. Currently, the Indian service sector is too dependent on the American business for its exports. This implies that India shall adopt a two-pronged strategy of Expand & Innovate, for the US and at global level.

An expansion in the US is only possible if one is able to adapt to the local concerns and is able to customise the service in a manner that it matches the expectations. However, the expansion alone is not going to serve India's interests for long, as other nations are also watching and are keen to jump in to take the advantage. China is catching up fast, and the language barrier is being taken apart brick by brick. Australia and New Zealand are becoming other big service exports destinations in services. India needs to innovate to remain ahead and relevant in the service exports. There are other countries such as Ireland, Philippines, Malaysia, Vietnam, Israel, South Africa, and the eastern European countries that are emerging as competitors for India in the space of IT service exports. Many of them have an advantage of cultural bonding, and some have the time zone advantage on their side; along with that they are focussing on upgrading their skill set and infrastructure.

The Indian companies can benefit from their early lead to set up knowledge and research hubs in the US and India to offer new innovative service solutions to the Americans. India needs to expand its service exports to other parts of the world. It has gained tremendous experience domestically and internationally to offer services to the South American and African continents. The Indian companies have advantages of cost, efficiency and experience of handling mass volume service requirements. If the American and Indian government can collaborate on service trade, the two nations can create a wide array of service bouquets for the developing nations.

The Indo-US collaboration and partnership can boost innovation and new service categories as well as revolutionise the digital world and e-Commerce across world. The biggest advantage of the Indo-US collaboration would be the merger of intellect, capital and markets. Together they can create such an eco-system, which not only fulfil the demand and requirements of their own nations as well as those of the other global markets. Artificial intelligence, 3D printing and robotics are going to transform the way humans live. The digital world is already influencing and bringing in behavioural changes in humans and will continue to far more greatly influence how the future of the humans evolve. There is no sphere left where the digital stamp is not imprinted – be it basic necessities like health, food, clothes or shelter, or leisure like entertainment, sports, or knowledge or travel or banking.

IT and digital services are influencing the way of governance; they are integral nowadays for smooth and transparent functioning of governments. They help anticipate, plan and respond through new Intelligent Integrated Service Grids, which look into traffic, water, power, communications, security, government-to-citizen (G2C), government-to-government (G2G), and government-to-business (G2B) interaction and other essential services like sanitation and municipal solid waste management services for the city. India can itself be a model for such service challenges and offer an opportunity to American as well as Indian companies to come up with solutions, which can help and be implemented in "India Smart Cities" project to make them more habitable and connected. These digital solutions and services can be replicated for the other developing nations.

Few of the opportunities in services where India and America can partner are listed, amongst the many more, where there is tremendous potential: information technology-business processing and management (IT-BPM), government services and administration, space and satellite, aviation – maintenance repairs and overhaul, banking, insurance & other financial services, entertainment and soft media content development, engineering, architectural and other design services, tourism, hospitality and travel services, healthcare, wellness and medical tourism, accounting and auditing services, legal services, education and skills training, logistics, etc.

Each of the above-mentioned service segments requires a carefully drafted and detailed approach between the two nations, keeping all stakeholders in the loop. We have tried to draw attention to a few of them to highlight the growth prospect they present.

1. Information Technology and Business Processing and Management (IT-BPM)

India is the global leader in the IT-BPM service exports sector. It is one of the few nations which have the capability and capacity to provide hardware, software as well as IT services. It has a robust and an excellent business delivery mechanism and is one of the most efficient (cost & quality) service providers in the world. The Indian IT services market is driven by testing services, custom application development and management (CADM), infrastructure services, consulting and system integration. The CADM demand is primarily driven by Social, Mobility, Analytics and Cloud (SMAC) technologies, responsible for modernising the legacy systems and causing a transformation in the system.[3] Within the IT-BPM sector, the IT services are being propelled by an increase in the usage of services pertaining to the adoption of SMAC, while BPM is driven by automation and analytics.

India is the fountainhead for budding start-ups, innovative and well-motivated. Many of these start-ups focus on emerging technologies, 3D printing, Internet of things, wearable devices, etc. They are well supported by many private venture capitalists (VC) from the US and are collaborating with larger firms to offer new solutions. With the increased need for automation, the threat in the coming years is expected to be on the reduction of human resource demand in the BPO industry and thus India losing a major advantage of its efficient work force. The new generation of entrepreneurs as well as already well-established players are well aware of such challenges and are trying to find innovative solutions for the same.

In India, the IT-BPM sector currently is one of the largest private sector employers with more than 3.7 million personnel, with over a one-third share of women employees. The majority of their operations is from non-metro cities in India, providing opportunity to young personnel from tier-2 and tier-3 cities. Over 1,70,000 foreign nationals are also employed within India in this sector.

As per a report in Forbes India, NASSCOM anticipates that the Indian IT-BPM industry is projected to grow at a rate of 8.6 per cent to reach over US$ 155 billion by the end of 2017.[4] With IT-BPM exports from India expected to reach US $118 billion,[5] the US and APAC are the fastest growing markets at 7.8 per cent, with a gradual stabilisation of growth in the European market. Retail, healthcare and travel and transportation have been the key verticals for the Indian IT-BPM industry, growing at the rate of 8 per cent.

IT-BPM is the sector which is most adversely impacted by the H1B visa restrictions. The IT outsourcing industry has been a beneficiary of the temporary US work visas (H1B) that are required by skilled foreign workers to work in that country. H1B visas are one of the most dominating modes in the Indian IT-BPM companies handling projects in the US. In this mode, employees of the IT-BPM companies are required to work on short-term and long-term projects onsite for a specific period of time depending on the needs of the project. It is one sector that many Americans believe has taken away the jobs of the Americans. The protectionist policies of the Trump administration and restrictions on data are going to hurt the industry more.

Contrary to perception that the Obama administration was soft on the Indian IT-BPM industry and was responsible for increasing unemployment, is nothing more than a myth. The Obama administration had already been restrictive on the H1B visas, despite the demands made by the American business houses to increase the H1B visas for India. The reality is that automation, artificial intelligence and robots are the reasons because of which even the Indian IT-BPM will have to re-skill its current workforce and the sector is evolving at such a fast pace that there are rapid changes in skill demand. What had been the key requirement 3-5 years back may be history by now, and to keep up with this fast change is not easy, as there have been massive burnouts that are making the workforce obsolete, unless they are re-skilled.

America had an advantage of outsourcing to India; not only it did not have to undertake such massive and expensive re-skill programs, it got ready-made solutions from Indian service exporters. The burden of re-skilling had to be taken up by the Indian companies. Having a very relative young population, from tier-2 and tier-3 cities, more needy, ambitious, agile, adjusting and equally skilled at a much lesser cost, gave India the edge. The factors of automation, AI and robots are also impacting the Indian companies but they undertake massive in-house training programmes and have prepared their workforce to multi-task and work simultaneously on multiple projects. The American business will need to learn a lot on this from the Indian companies. This is the reason why we feel there is a complementary role.

An estimated amount of US$2 billion annually is contributed by the employees on H1B visas to the US social security system as they stay in the US for short time (minimum time limit required to seek benefits under the US social security system is 10 years – a huge chunk of this amount is neither utilised by, nor refunded to them and is going straight to the US kitty to its advantage, whereas the US nationals working in India and their employers, on the completion of 58 years of age, get back a large part of these contributions from their provident fund (PF) account. The contribution made by the US nationals to the PF benefits them eventually, whereas the Indians working in the US lose out on their rightful dues. Both the governments are aware of the situation. It is evident that the US is at a clear advantage here and wishes to continue on same path as it suits it. So, if the US is keen on further restrictions on H1B visas, it shall also have to clear the dues of the Indians, which it pockets. Or the Indian government can come up with a legislation for reform in the PF, where it can restrict any benefit being paid back to foreigners.

Re-skill shall be the focus of the Indian government and of the Indian IT-BPM industry, otherwise in few years India will be laden with educated resources but obsolete at a young age. It is difficult to control the pace of technology nowadays; especially when everyday there are new services with new features being launched. The pioneers of today can be big losers tomorrow. Yahoo, Blackberry, Nokia, etc. are few classic examples who changed the ways of industry when they were at their prime, now they are struggling. The face of retailing has changed, and so does the way of payment with digital moneys (no credit cards required now). In such a scenario, the focus has to be on continuous skill upgradation as it will also help in retaining loyal employees and increase productivity and diversification in the newer segments of service exports.

The Indian government must push for the introduction of computers and digital world at a young age in all schools, especially the government administered schools. The introduction to softwares, languages and codes, graphics, 3D, CAD-CAM, etc. shall be part of the curriculum, with more advanced levels being introduced in colleges and professional institutes. This will prepare the young children for tomorrow's digital world, and also ensure that the Indian strength is continued.

It's no secret that currently few of the degrees granted by some private universities are not recognised even within India, further affecting the credibility of the Indian education system and the employability of the people. The quality and standards of professional education can be improved through a proper accreditation process. In almost all the cases, companies in the services sector have to invest substantially in the training of their employees in the absence of any organised availability of trained professionals. The government can work with service exporters and educational institutes on a public–private partnership basis to identify the skill requirements and to design the appropriate academic courses and training programmes to facilitate skill development. A focus on vocational training and development of appropriate curriculum will increase the employability of students in the services sector.

It is strongly recommend for opening up of the education and professional training institutes for 100 per cent FDI from the reputed American universities and colleges. It will provide an opportunity for Indians to be at par with American peers in terms of practical as well as theoretical experience. It will also increase the employability of Indians in the American MNC companies.

The Indian IT industry has been catering to worldwide demands by developing more BPOs within the country to deliver across the value chain. The major challenges faced by the Indian outsourcing providers are data privacy and data security. There have been breaches and concerns have been raised on the same; this limits the growth of business. This implies that there is a need for a detailed data privacy and security legislation in India, which may be useful for accessing more businesses from the US and the EU. The US could be helpful in providing inputs like technology (soft and hard) and help India in formulation of the policy.

Moving up the value chain in IT services, the focus of Indian start-ups shall be on providing solutions for key trends in engineering, research and development, like environment protection and tracking, power and energy efficient usage systems and saving devices, medical devices and wellness trackers, virtual reality and experiential solutions, wearable gadgets, logistics, transportation, security and surveillance, eyeball gazing and analytics for retail, intelligent traffic systems, 3D printing etc. The US market and other markets like the EU, Japan etc., are developed and ready to accept them.

With India strengthening its position in the IT-BPM arena, many start-ups are offering innovative and disruptive technologies for new sectors, including smart healthcare, smart cities, smart infrastructure, etc. These technologies have the ability to power the next mega trend globally. The US companies can help and partner with the Indian start-ups that weave together a number of ideas and thoughts into a more mutually beneficial Indo-US relationship.

2. Government Services and Administration

The biggest service consumers and providers in the world are the government and government administrative bodies, and this is one service sector which is deciding the future of the existence of every government in the world, as the citizens of the world are not only looking forward to good governance, they wish to see it transparent, responsive, fast and lively to their issues. The level of interaction has reached a new crescendo, wherein IT, Telecommunications and Media have played a critical role and are now well entrenched to a greater degree in most developed nations, and are getting more integrated in the developing nations and are in process of implementation in other poor nations. The aspiration of a nation and the pride of a nation depend upon the service it can provide to its citizens along with safety and security. The nations where the service level is at the highest are also the most developed nations with a high standard of living, and where it is poor, the nations are lagging behind economically, socially, culturally as well on health, education and human rights.

Apart from setting and providing urban and rural infrastructure, the governments across the world are responsible for providing the following basic services (apart from security and law and order):

- Government Services to the Citizens (G2C), which cover services like electricity, sanitation, drinking water, transport network, education, healthcare, telecommunications, etc.
- Government services for Business (G2B) which covers services like banking and insurance, currency valuation and exchange, taxes and other levies, financial controls and regulations, etc.
- Government-to-Government (G2G) which covers services being exchanged between two or more departments of the government, or between local governments, or from state to central government, like security and surveillance, taxation subsidies and grants, governance, etc.

The South American, African and Asian continents have a majority of the developing and poor nations. There is huge gap in services demand and delivery in these nations. India has very close ties with them as it is also transforming from a developing nation to a developed one. India can leverage its learning and help these nations to improve upon or altogether build new services so that these nations too can benefit from India's experience and learning.

This is one service sector, where in the American service providers can help India. India faces many challenges; the same can be easily resolved and supported by the American service experts. It is an opportunity for the Trump administration to guide and work along with the Indian government, especially on the smart city projects, where such services would be of great value to the Indians. The Indian government shall be more forthcoming for such service imports and must facilitate either through business to business collaborations or can go to the length of creating a SPV and collaborate directly, and thus build strength for itself.

Not only the Americans have the opportunity to offer their services in India, they also have the opportunity to forge new alliances here and through India to build a base from where it can provide further services to Asia, Africa and the West Asian countries. It can build capacity not only for India, but utilise the available pool of talent to further expand its business, and that too at a much efficient cost. India has the capacity to build and launch satellites; these are important for satellite mapping, weather predictions, emergency response planning during natural disasters, global positioning and geo-tagging of the government assets, etc. In addition to these, information technology, telecommunications, designing, engineering and architectural skills play a very large role in such services. The American companies can benefit from same in India, as all these are abundantly available at a much younger age as well as at a lesser cost.

Electrical power distribution planning, designing, operations, maintenance and energy saving is one of the key challenges for power-deficient nations. Smart grids, integration with renewable power generation sources and effective grid management skills are required. Both the American and Indian companies can come together and capture such markets. India is one of the most populated countries with a very high density of population in cities. Its experience and understanding of mass connect, management is unparalleled, especially at a fraction of costs, than what the develop nations spend.

China has realised the potential of such services and have taken a leadership role in helping other nations in setting such service networks in Africa and also in Asia. It has already put into action its ambitious "One

Road One Belt" project, through which it is trying not only to offer its services and funds for development in countries like Pakistan, Nepal etc., but also through them, is pushing its goods exports and security agenda. Through its agreements China has got a strong hold on many of the natural resources in the African countries, which they supply to China.

India and America are the largest democracies of the world; they both provide funds for many of social, health and infrastructural development programmes. They can help the developing nations more by providing more of such services through these funds or those of the UN-sponsored programmes. India has very good cultural, historical, social and trade relations with them, hence both American and Indian companies can benefit from such initiatives.

The Indian government should invite American experts in civic services to have their base in India, and offer them tasks in smart city projects. The government can facilitate them by creating a special service zone for them with complete infrastructure. Both India and America will gain a great deal, and objectives set by both the nations can be supported and complimented by the other.

3. Aviation-Maintenance Repairs and Overhauling (MRO)

The air travel demand has increased steadily over the last 50 years. More than a luxury, it has become a necessity, and is counted as one of the essential services for the nation. Currently, India is the ninth largest civil aviation market in the world with a market size of USD 16 billion and aims to become the third largest market by 2020.[6] India is also one of the fastest-growing aviation markets in the world with a growth of 18 per cent in the throughput of international and domestic passengers over the last financial year reaching a total passenger throughput of 224 million. Cargo throughput increased by 7 per cent to 2.7 million tonnes during the same period, while air traffic movements for the period was 1.79 million, which is an increase of 12 per cent over the same period last year.[7]

Globally, from period of 1980 onwards, the passenger traffic has grown at a 5 per cent CAGR. The trend is expected to continue and has led to an increased demand for aircrafts. Boeing estimates that from 2015 to

2034, the number of new aircrafts delivered globally would be 38,050 with 38 per cent of the demand from Asia alone.[8] The accelerated rate of new aircraft deliveries will result in a massive technology shift over the period. By 2027, 58 per cent of the fleet will be new-generation aircraft.[9]

The American aircraft manufacturer Boeing dominates with over 40 per cent market share (wide body) in India. It sources more than half a billion dollars' worth of components and services from 30 direct and over 100 indirect suppliers in India. The value of sourcing is expected to double by the year 2020. Most of the airlines in India are on an aggressive growth path with their fleets being relatively new. These airlines mostly fly abroad for their MRO requirements to destinations such as Singapore. They lose time and money in the process as currently India lacks such a facility. However, going forward, with the fleet aging, the MRO market has ample scope for the US companies to set up MRO operations in India to serve the large market in India and also to the neighbourhood nations.

The MRO sector mainly incorporates companies providing services in repairs, inspection or modification and overhauling of the aircraft components. This service segment is split and recognised on the nature of the core services provided by them, that is, airframe maintenance, engine maintenance, line maintenance and component maintenance. MRO in the aviation sector is further divided by the type of aircraft: civil aviation MRO and defence aviation MRO. As an initial step, civil aviation MRO is crucial from the trade perspective.

The Indian civil aviation MRO market is at a nascent stage currently and its market size of India is projected at US$1.9 billion in 2017 and is expected to grow to US$3.5 billion by 2027. Commercial airline MRO global growth will be healthy at 3.8 per cent CAGR over the 10-year period, growing from the current demand of US$75.6 billion in 2017 to just over US$109 billion by 2027.[10]

On an average, every airline spends almost 13-15 per cent of its revenues towards maintenance, repairs and overhaul, making MRO the second highest cost item after fuel; this is common insight from the aviation industry. The growth of the MRO industry in India is severely restricted due to challenges such as a disadvantageous tax regime and lack of adequate space and infrastructure at airports. The MRO industry is at a nascent stage in India, mostly dependent on MRO services from other nations; approximately 90 per cent or above of the MRO services and expenditures are incurred in countries like Sri Lanka, the UAE, Singapore, etc. India's share is a meagre 1 per cent of the Global MRO Market and a lack of MRO facilities in India is a prime reason for that.[11]

This presents significant opportunities for the US companies, and the aviation sector growth in India augurs well for them across the aerospace and MRO value chain which can grow in the Indian market or utilise the cost efficiencies and engineering skills India has to offer. The American companies can utilise the cost efficiencies and engineering manpower of India in the global MRO and aerospace supply chain

This service sector in India faces a shortage of skilled manpower and this creates difficulties for it to adhere to strict quality requirements of global aerospace and MRO companies. A development of skilled talent is required in the field. To enable skill development, the government could collaborate with the industry and academic institutes to formulate MRO-specific skill development training modules, by incorporating international best practices. The governments of both the US and India along with the private sector should work on bridging this skill gap.

The MRO sector in India has long suffered due to lack of policy support, excessive taxation, high airport charges, painful procedures for customs clearances for imported parts, etc. The US companies and policymakers can help India with their learning and experience and help the Indian MRO industry to grow. The reforms from the Indian central and state governments are expected to ease the stated bottlenecks. Few of the steps are already in the process of being undertaken as are some others. The following examples are recommended for the growth of the MRO service sector:

- Exemptions from custom duty on the imports of tools, equipment, spare parts, etc., as required for the MRO services. The US and Indian governments can have a bilateral agreement on the same.
- The government could reduce taxations on the MRO services at central and state levels, enabling the MRO companies based in India to offer globally competitive pricing.

- Custom clearance is another bottleneck, where delays happen; projects get delayed and become expensive in operation. Simplification and standardisation of custom clearance process for import of equipment, tools, components, etc., required in MRO infrastructure and services will enable a timely availability of tools and machinery.
- The Indian government could ensure that adequate space is mandatorily allocated at the Indian airports for MRO.
- Indian and the American public ltd and private R&D agencies could be motivated to collaborate or enter into new joint ventures to build capability and capacity and for developing the necessary technologies.
- Building globally competitive skills and capabilities: Only a limited number of players have mandatory global certifications from the US Federal Aviation Administration (FAA) or the European Aviation Safety Agency (EASA) or the UAE's General Civil Aviation Authority (GCAA), for carrying out heavy maintenance works for aircraft. The Indian government could promote certifications by offering sponsorship or reimbursement of the cost of obtaining global certifications as an incentive to the industry.
- The MRO service sector infrastructure is capital-intensive, and it will help the growth of this sector if the Indian government through its policy framework can make available affordable finance for setting up the MRO facilities and their development.
- A liberalisation of 100 per cent FDI shall be permitted to invest in and establish the required infrastructure in this service sector.
- The government can also enter into strategic partnerships with other neighbouring countries, ensuring that not only the domestic requirement is efficiently managed, saving important revenue, but also India could also tap the ASEAN countries such as Singapore, UAE, Sri Lanka, Malaysia and Philippines. These countries are important trade hubs for India, besides being geographically closer.

4. Banking, Insurance and Other Financial Services

Services like Paytm, mobile payment banks, internet banking, digital payment, debit and credit cards on mobile, Aadhar-based payment gateways (BHIM) are changing the ways banking used to happen. They are disrupting the archaic financial services and banking infrastructure; democratising and simplifying information, unbundling services and customising them, causing financial disintermediation and reducing the exclusivity of financial services.

The transition is going to be far more rapid in the near future, so much so that the entire traditional system of the banking process is getting challenged. This presents an excellent opportunity to new start-ups to introduce new disruptive ways of banking. The role of bank branches is getting limited and ATM kiosks are becoming more interactive and efficient. With more internet reach and far deeper smartphone penetration across India, it is driving customer preference for tech-enabled banking services and is a clear opportunity for companies with concentration and capabilities in tech-based, internet-based and mobile-based financial service offering.

India has the potential to become the fifth largest banking industry in the world by 2020 and the third largest by 2025.[12] The Indian banking sector assets reached 1.96 trillion USD in FY15 from 1.3 trillion USD in FY10, with over 70 per cent accounted for by the public sector. The RBI's push, as well as implementation of schemes such as the Pradhan Mantri Jan Dhan Yojana, which connect and make banking accessible to every household in India, connect them to financial service networks. There is an opportunity for retail banks to reach out with their services to the newly banked population of 218 million and the unbanked population of 197 million. As of May 2016, MFIs, Payment Banks and PPIs were skilled to serve small ticket-size transactions in a cost efficient manner and the banks were ready to invest and grow their network in the rural and semi-urban space.

The Indian banking system consists of 26 public sector banks, 20 private sector banks, 43 foreign banks, 56 regional rural banks, 1,589 urban cooperative banks and 93,550 rural cooperative banks, in addition to cooperative credit institutions. There are four major US banks with a total of 49 branches operating in India (American Express Banking Corporation, Bank of America, Citibank and JP Morgan Chase). Two of the US banks have presence through a representative office (Bank of New York Mellon and Wells Fargo). Citibank has the most significant presence in the Indian banking sector amongst other the US banks with 42 banking branches of the total 49 branches operated by the US banks. The total capital employed by Citigroup in banking business in India is in excess of US$3 billion.[13]

India is still largely an underinsured nation with huge demand in every insurance product segment to be tapped, be it health, vehicle, general, property, natural calamities, etc. Despite the presence of more than 50 insurance companies, a low level of insurance penetration presents a significant opportunity for the US banking and financial institutes.

The American financial institutes and banks have an excellent opportunity in India now, when mobile and internet penetration has reached every corner of the nation. They can partner with Indian banks and other start-ups to reach these newly financially connected people. The demand for insurance products, mutual funds, saving instruments, investments, loans, etc. is waiting to be tapped. Currently, there is limited presence of US insurers in the Indian market, though the potential of the market is manifold.

For the American banks and financial institutions to come and invest in India, it is important to bring in banking reforms in India; obviously, without compromising the security and the risks involved. The current regulation structure is hindering the real potential of the American banks, and the role that they can play in the development of India.

- The RBI and the Indian government can decide on applications at a faster pace for the American banks after a thorough evaluation. A new bilateral treaty can be signed between India and the US to facilitate the establishment of American banks and financial institutions in India. The terms can be mutually agreed upon and discussed to safeguard the interests of both nations.
- India needs to resolve the issue of local incorporation of the American banks as it may lead to a change in their business and operating model. Currently, all the foreign banks operate as branches in India. The Indian government should evaluate the possibility of issuing differential licences or graded licences to the

US banks and financial institutes depending on their business models with a particular player focussing on a specific product, geography or market segment.

- Many of the American banks have niche products and offer them to their niche clients. They face challenges from the guidelines of the priority sector lending under which foreign banks are supposed to lend a substantial share to the priority sectors, which alters their business model, and acts as a hindrance. The Indian government and RBI can form new policies so that such niche banks can also be set up in India. This experience would also help the Indian banks to come up with their range of specialised and tailored services.
- Certain priority sectors requiring huge capital push especially in housing, healthcare infrastructure, smart city projects, large infrastructure projects like metro rail, logistics infrastructure, etc. can be opened up for the US financial institutes. Both the Indian and the US governments can be party to it and safeguard their interests and resolve any issue.
- The FDI in insurance brokering shall be raised to 100 per cent to push a deeper penetration of the insurance products. The current insurance penetration is around half of the global standards and is very dismal when compared to the developed nations.

The collaboration between the Indian and the US companies could be a model for other developing nations especially in Africa, South America and Asia.

5. Engineering, Architectural and Other Design Services

India's exports in architectural and engineering services are roughly estimated at US$10 million. India's exports in the engineering design and development sector are growing rapidly with deeper inroads into the global engineering space. With new softwares and computer hardware that can support complex calculations for design validation through computer modelling and creating virtual reality, the Indian engineers and architects are now providing end-to-end solutions in design. The task of engineering now can be divided into different modules that can be outsourced while the principal design or engineering firm concentrates on its core activities. It has enhanced the efficiency of the firm, improved processes, led to cost advantage and lowered time-to-market for the product. The Indian Engineering Services Outsourcing (ESO) has become a new segment of the Indian outsourcing industry.

In the engineering service exports, hi-tech manufacturing and automotive industries are the major markets contributing 75 per cent of the total revenues, and aerospace is set to be the sunrise industry over the next decade.[14] The task of engineering design has vastly transformed following the introduction of Computer Aided Engineering (CAE), which comprises of Computer Aided Design (CAD), Computer Aided Analysis (CAA), Computer Integrated Manufacturing (CIM), Computer Aided Manufacturing (CAM), Material Requirement Planning (MRP), and Computer Aided Planning (CAP). These tools have helped the Indian engineers and architects to be at par with global talent. The tools help create models, test them and validate the design without any physical prototype being built. It saves lots of costs as well as is more accurate as the minutest of the factors are captured and analysed through these tools.

India is not only is an outsourcing destination for engineering and architectural services but is also a large market in itself, which adds to its advantage, as more global players are interested in India for reasons beyond the cost advantage. With the Indian government focusing on creating robust infrastructure for India, and its commitment to develop 100 smart cities in the immediate future, it makes sense for the US engineering, design and architectural firms to collaborate and set up base in India. Not only would they be able to cater to their own domestic requirements, but also would be able to reach out to other Asian and African nations.

Despite the opportunity and the intent for growth of trade in engineering and architectural services, they suffer from trade restrictions and barriers put in by both India as well as the US; hence, losing out on golden opportunities in both the nations and at the global level. The benefit of such restrictions goes straight to the European and Chinese firms which currently have the leadership in such services. A classic example is India's

Architects Act, 1972 where as per the letter and spirit of the Architects Act, foreign architects can be engaged or hired as architects in India only if they are registered with the Council of Architects (COA) or through a Mutual Recognition Agreement (MRA) between the COA and the home country regulator of the foreign architect. Otherwise, foreign architects can be engaged only as consultants or as designers with the prior permission of the central government [Section 37(1) (b), Architect Act, 1972]. It is also contrary to other provisions like that while the opening statement of Section 25 of the Architects Act requires only residency, paragraph (c) limits registration to only the citizens of India. This anomaly under Section 25 needs to be corrected by the Indian government and the COA.

Similarly, while the US wishes India to open its market for its professionals, very hypocritically, it continues to obstruct and create new barriers for the Indian professionals and the companies wishing to provide their services to American market. The effort has to be reciprocal and one country can't be expected to roll over the other. Any concern on their competencies and capabilities needs to be addressed mutually and an accreditation system can be followed in both the nations to ensure that the rightful concerns have been addressed. MRAs need to strategically mapped and implemented. If need be, both the nations must create a framework to find gaps and anomalies in their education system, so that resources on both end are well trained and compatible and in understanding of local bye-laws and other compliance requirements.

As India seeks recognition of its professionals through registration in foreign countries, it is imperative that the requirement of registration in India is made consistent with international leading practices. Several developed countries require that an individual passes a Professional Practice Examination (PPE) to make him/her eligible for registration. The Architects Act, 1972 does not require such an exam for registration. The PPE may be introduced for registration. This shall also help to improve the prospects of entering into MRAs.

The one very critical aspect of engineering and architectural services export is the role played by computer softwares. Most of the design softwares are developed and imported to India at very high costs. The effort needs to develop upgraded Indian softwares which can help in increasing faster calculations and more creativity.

6. Tourism, Hospitality and Travel Services

The tourism sector is one of India's largest services sectors and a key contributor to India's economic development and employment generation. The World Travel & Tourism Council calculated that tourism in India generated US$220 billion or 9.6 per cent of its GDP in 2016 and supported 40.343 million jobs – 9.3 per cent of its total employment. The sector is predicted to grow at an annual rate of 6.8 per cent to US$440 billion by 2027 (10% of the GDP).[15] The sector encompasses travel, tourist attractions, travel agents and tour operators along with hospitality infrastructure like hotels, inns, cafeterias, restaurants, etc. In tourism, exports transpire when foreign tourists visit India and utilise services provided by partakers in the sector. Tourism is one of the top generators of foreign exchange and its performance influences directly other sectors such as hospitality, food and beverage, retail and recreational services.

About 8.89 million foreign tourists arrived in India in 2016 compared to 8.027 million in 2015, recording a growth of 10.7 per cent.[16] As per the UNWTO report, approximately 1.2 billion people travelled abroad in the year 2015.[17] This means that India's share has been a very low 0.7 per cent of the global travel share. This highlights the fact that India has a lot of ground to cover to get featured amongst the top countries in international tourism.

The *Travel & Tourism Competitiveness Report 2017* ranks India 40th out of 136 countries overall. The report ranks the price competitiveness of India's tourism sector as 10th, out of 136 countries. It mentions that India ranks for air transport as 32nd. India scored high on natural and cultural resources at rank 9.

According to the US National Travel and Tourism Office, in 2016, a total of 66.9 million US citizens travelled outside the country[18] and around 1.3 million US tourists arrived in India (growth of 27 per cent over the previous 4 years),[19] i.e. hardly 1.8 per cent of the US citizens travel to India. Looked at from the perspective of the next 10 years' growth in the

American tourists travelling abroad, it is more critical for the Indian tourism sector to capture that market. Similarly, Indian tourists in the US spent more than US$13 billion in 2016 as a US export in the travel and tourism sector.[20] The tourism sector is critical for both the nations and it would help them grow economically if it is promoted further mutually by India and the US.

India has 28 world heritage sites and 25 bio-geographic zones; the Ministry of Tourism is broadening its tourism scope through new products, such as rural, adventure, wellness, medical and eco-tourism with an objective to increase the inflow of tourists in the country. Yet, there is a constant struggle to provide an efficient, attractive and sustainable tourism ecosystem and infrastructure. The biggest handicap is again of heavy capital investment that this sector requires, and shortage of required skill set. There is a tremendous opportunity for the American companies at every stage of this sector, from planning, designing, implementation & construction, maintenance and operations, to training and investment, etc.

The US companies can collaborate or form joint ventures with Indian companies to develop sound infrastructure in the form of amenities for tourists to provide them with an enjoyable experience at existing and new destinations all across the country. The Indian government has already permitted 100 per cent FDI in tourism and the US companies can take advantage of same.

The Indian government can also undertake action on the following recommendations:

- Map the destination and the foreign tourists that visit them, understand their nationality, their requirements and other such characteristics. For the US which is India's biggest tourism export market, mapping for each US state shall be undertaken to understand their needs in depth, which can be supported back in India.
- Compare India's competitiveness with other international tourist destinations for each type of tourist, and build on strengths to improve competition and bridge the gaps to attract more tourists to these destinations in India.

- Mapping helps in understanding the demography of the foreign tourists, and it can help companies develop the leisure and hospitality facilities – matching and appealing to their tastes. India needs to create an all-round experience for a variety of tourist categories: along with the development of sightseeing sites, efforts shall be made to provide an all-round experience to tourists through trained, certified and experienced multilingual tour guides, children's interests, availability of food outlets offering international cuisines, etc. A pleasurable stay would surely invite more visits to the destination through word-of-mouth publicity and increase the chances of repeat arrivals.
- Develop and maintain a variety of tourist destinations within the country that could offer choices and options to tourists. Cleanliness and upkeep of tourist sites have to be given the utmost importance.
- Budget and invest heavily on the support structure that facilitates tourist movement within the country. All important tourist destinations must be connected through roads, railways and airports to facilitate easy access. The government can also permit the same through PPP (Public Private Partnership) or through joint ventures. Air connectivity to non-metros is extremely low, especially in the North-East region and hilly terrains of the country which have tremendous potential for international tourism. The focus shall be air connectivity through no-frills airports and Greenfield projects through PPP or FDI.
- Soft infrastructure is likewise imperative in improving the overall tourism ecosystem in a country. Clean facilities, safety and security requirements are essential and cannot be more emphasised, when so many undesirable incidents have occurred with foreign tourists, especially with women. The accessibility to safe drinking water and hygienic food is an elementary requirement of a tourist, along with clean and hygienic sanitary facilities and amenities. The creation of special Tourist Safety & Assistance force (TSA) can help instil faith in the foreign tourists.
- Efforts shall be put in for payment and other transactional requirements and procedures through the digital medium, cashless modes, etc., wherein the tourists are able to compare the payments with their local currency.

- Skill development to make the sector more conducive for foreign tourists. Language and other soft skills are critical and can be provided through government programmes. There is a need for increased focus on grooming, on-the-job training and communication skills, courses in foreign languages and standardisation and monitoring of curricula in private institutions.
- Invite greater private participation in archaeological and heritage tourism
- Promote new forms of tourism: While the government has been promoting India as a tourist destination, new forms of tourism could be separately highlighted as adventure tourism, inland water cruise or sea cruise, water-themed destinations and underwater tourism, wellness tourism, rural lifestyle glimpse, eco-tourism, niche market for physically challenged and senior citizens, entertainment, music or art-oriented, films, etc.
- India has been the fountainhead of many of the prominent religions still followed across the world. India has many destinations which have deep religious connection with these religions. India must focus on developing these destinations for the purposes of religious tourism.
- Facilitate the arrival and travel of foreign tourists to make travel of foreign tourists easier and more convenient. Cultural and linguistic considerations could be kept in mind while developing amenities and tourism infrastructure. Visa on arrival for a short period for all countries except for enemy states should be provided. Apart from sensitive areas, all airports near tourist destinations shall have immigration and emigration counters to facilitate tourists.
- Special trains for foreign tourists with best of amenities like Wi-Fi, upgraded toilets, e-catering services etc. along with a cultural tinge in trains across India.
- Promote Indian destinations in popular soap operas, reality shows, events and other soap programmes in countries where India wishes to promote Indian tourism and appoint ex-servicemen and trained volunteers at major tourist spots.
- Stress on the need for accreditation of Indian service providers and their compliance to best practices in the International tourism

industry. International quality certifications build a positive perception and acceptance of the quality offered by Indian firms, making them more appealing to prospective tourists.

- Participation in international events: Events and exhibitions are an effective platform to promote tourism services (offered by firms) in other countries. Events held by the government (in various countries) and trade bodies could be leveraged.
- Extensive marketing and promotional campaigns across all key markets through all-media platforms including the use of a professional public relations agency, to connect stakeholders and educate the market. Customised and targeted campaigns can be created to reach niche tourists through social media, radio and outdoor mediums.
- Encourage private–public collaboration and sponsorship through CSR initiatives. Indian museums, galleries, etc., need a quantum leap to create more experiential and engaging exhibits and environment. The government can invite corporates through their CSR initiatives to sponsor maintenance and upkeep of historical monuments and for the development and maintenance of museums across the country.

7. Healthcare, Wellness and Medical Tourism

Healthcare is not only crucial from the perspective of providing good health to the citizens, but is one of the key parameters that drive the economic and social growth of the country. A healthy society ensures high productivity, longer and healthy life, a happier, literate and socially secure country. It stimulates consumption and production.

In India, the healthcare sector is the fifth largest employer among all the sectors, with medical education sector being one of the largest in the world. Indian doctors and their knowledge and skills are well recognised worldwide. The alternative medicine practices like Ayurveda, Siddha, Unani, Naturopathy and Homoeopathy are also strong in India. As per the written reply given in 2016 by Shri Shripad Yesso Naik (Minister of State, Independent Charge for AYUSH), there are 7,71,468 AYUSH registered practitioners throughout the country as on January 1, 2016 who contribute to AYUSH healthcare services in the country.[21]

The awareness level as well as service levels in the healthcare ecosystem have seen a tremendous positive change, and are witnessing the emergence of new service delivery models through the use of innovative technologies and telecommunication systems. The focus of the people has shifted from providing cure for ailments to maintaining an overall wellness/fitness level. The Internet of Things (IoT) has helped in integrating technology, gadgets and wearable detectors to collect health data of the person/patient and communicate with physicians in real time. There is a clear visible shift from the old traditional way to a new innovative approach. It has opened new access to diagnosis and transformed the patient-physician relationship. It has helped create new business models for the delivery of healthcare. Old traditional business models and operating processes may no longer deliver the expected services to the rising demands of patients.

The consumption of healthcare services is growing globally and is evolving with new trends, such as medical tourism and e-health. A new pattern has developed with patients from developed nations like the US travelling for health services to developing nations like India, owing to the low costs, easy information availability on the internet and relatively smaller waiting periods. Many countries are also providing healthcare services through the telemedicine mode to countries in need of the same. Emerging markets, such as India, Thailand and Malaysia, are driving the supply side of cross-border healthcare services.[22]

India has emerged as a hub for medical tourism with quality healthcare services at an affordable price. Over the last decade, India has seen a quantum jump in people coming to India from the US and other developed nations for medical services. To them, India offers an attractive value proposition with multispecialty private healthcare services being provided to them at a fraction of the costs in comparison to their home countries, without or lower waiting times in hospitals for admission and treatment in comparison to their own nation. India's cost arbitrage gives it an advantage over other countries offering similar services, such as Singapore and Malaysia, and saves about 30 to 70 per cent of the costs by getting services in India. The presence of highly qualified and world-recognised doctors, nurses and other healthcare staff make Indian healthcare services attractive to them. India has attained a leadership position in complex medical procedures and skills in advanced healthcare in cardiovascular, eye, neurological and organ transplants procedures with a high success rate.

Telemedicine, offshoring transcriptions, diagnosis consultations, etc. are few of the other services where India excels; its digital innovations and technology are revolutionising the entire healthcare sector. The role of technology and telecommunication is being incorporated in every aspect of the healthcare delivery value chain. The global healthcare market recognises India as amongst the leading hubs in the Asian countries for offshoring transcription services owing to its infrastructure, availability of skilled manpower and a favourable economic environment.

The US healthcare system is currently stretched and under pressure due to long waiting period for many lifestyle-related ailments and also due to its dependency on insurance system. Many of the ailments are not generally covered under insurance for example dental care, eyesight, surgeries related to beauty, physiotherapy, old age care, etc. These services are much cheaper in India and popular among medical tourists from the US. An increasing emphasis on physical and mental health has propelled India's wellness market to grow.

To further expand these services for the US nationals, India shall engage the US administration more deeply and put across a framework through collaboration, accreditation, certification, etc., to assure the American patients getting at-par treatment as they would get in the US. There is wide scope for the US companies to expand their business in India by setting up new hospitals, providing diagnostic infrastructure and cutting-edge technology in surgery and use of robotics in healthcare. They understand the American needs deeper and can match their expectations in India in a much more cost-efficient manner. The Indian government can push by permitting 100 per cent FDI in this sector and also allotting land and other such resources for American business. It will also help Indians to have more access to the healthcare system.

India needs investments in expanding its healthcare infrastructure to tier-2, 3 cities urgently. The American companies can help in creating such infrastructure and simultaneously benefit from it. The US can also help in improving in medical ambulance services and the design and expansion of such services across the nation. A large number of new chain of labs and diagnostic centres are required, which can be established by the US healthcare service providers.

Air ambulances are required and can be an excellent business opportunity and a bridge between India and the US healthcare system as well as promoting more medical tourism in India.

8. Accounting and Auditing Services

In the last few decades, rapid industrialisation and business expansion has occurred worldwide, especially in the developing nations resulting in an increase in the global demand for accounting and auditing services. It has increased significantly because of increased international trade activities, and regularly changing global accounting and auditing standards. An organisation with business interests in different parts of the world needs consistent systems and processes. It needs a consistent accounting and auditing system. This has led to the evolution of a global accounting and auditing network. These MNCs also need to abide and comply with the local legal framework and auditing standards to avoid any litigation or risks. This has increase the demand for expertise in international auditing firms.

These factors are the main driving forces behind the growing demand for these services. Owing to the substantial base of low-cost talent pool and technology-driven outsourcing capabilities, India has emerged as a preferred destination for business in the auditing sector.

India as a nation itself is witnessing a significant growth in multinational footprints and a growing start-up ecosystem resulting in opportunities for Indian as well as other multinational auditing firms in India. The adoption of the new Indian Accounting Standards (Ind AS), congregated with the International Financial Reporting Standards (IFRS) and the Institute of Chartered Accountants of India (ICAI), has encouraged the demand for the Indian chartered accountant professionals. The demand is primarily from regions where the English language and the accounting system is similar; the Indian professionals are not only providing services in the EU, but also in the West Asian countries and neighbouring countries like Nepal, Bangladesh, Sri Lanka, and also to Australia and Singapore.

The accounting and auditing sector in India is significantly fragmented and comprises largely of small and medium-sized firms which limits their growth internationally. Developed economies, such as the US, the UK, France, Netherlands and the Gulf nations are home to several large auditing firms having a global reach and footprint. They have an early mover advantage as well as having established systems and processes that comply with global accounting and auditing standards. They have also strengthened their portfolio by creating a bouquet of services which offer them research and analysis, market intelligence and insight into the best practices being adopted worldwide. These large firms have an advantage of the economies of scale, and focus on expanding industry-specific knowledge and technical expertise. These firms have invested extensively to develop the required tools and skills to meet the market's demands for high quality services. These large network firms compete aggressively in terms of industry expertise, reputation, quality and cost.

Global audit firms enjoy a reputational advantage with companies, which is one of the factors allowing them to charge a significantly higher fee as compared to other mid and small-sized audit firms. The clients look for credibility and domain expertise while hiring auditing firms. The Indian audit firms need to concentrate on building good relations with their clients and establish their brand name in the domestic and international market.

The US accounting and auditing firms have tremendous opportunity in India; not only India is a large market for them, but it also becomes a destination for outsourcing through which the American firms can be more cost-efficient. They have able support from Indian professionals and can help increase their penetration level in other developing nations.

India can also benefit from the presence of these American auditing firms, as they bring with them huge experience and understanding of best practices being followed across other nations and across all manufacturing and service domains. It helps the Indian accounting and auditing firms with the strategies to cope with future challenges and build up their expertise fast enough to exploit the global opportunities

The Indian and the US governments must set up a robust mechanism for the recognition and accreditation of the accounting and auditing firms. The markets shall be opened up mutually and barriers brought down. Few of the recommendations are listed below to build a strong base for service trade in this sector:

- Restrictions can be eased off on international payments, which create an obstacle for export services.
- Ease in visa for the mobility of Indian audit professionals for exploring global opportunities.
- Barriers to be removed for ensuring an easy transfer of technology and information systems to encourage IT system calibration.
- Training and skill enhancement for a better understanding of global accounting and auditing systems. The adoption of global best practices is needed.
- Differing professional certification requirements create barriers for the entry of Indian audit professionals; the US companies can help remove such anomalies through accreditation, certification or by suggesting the change required within the Indian system.
- Significant differences among accounting practices across nations leads to differing accounting norms and lack of standardisation in accounting practices. Hence, it is important to understand the compliance norms, quality standards etc. The US companies can help through training.
- Relaxation in allowing FDI in accounting and auditing services is expected to provide greater exposure to the Indian firms and boost their potential to export services
- Easing of the restriction of '20 companies per auditor in a year' rule for an audit firm that might allow auditors to provide services to more than 20 clients in a year. Reforms in this regulation shall boost MSMEs in the accounting and auditing sector, as they get a major portion of their work from unlisted companies.
- Amending the Chartered Accountants Act, 1949 to permit multinational firms to conduct audit activities in India, without the need for collaboration with domestic associates.

9. Legal Services

The legal service market includes services such as advisory, representation, documentation and procedures across diverse areas of law, including corporate, criminal, real estate and labour. India has 6,00,000 legal professionals in the world – the second-highest after the US. Owing to the expertise of professionals in domains such as arbitration, competition law, environmental law, international trade law, outbound foreign direct investment, restructuring and insolvency, the Indian legal firms have performed well and are sought in India as well as in other nations.

There was a surge in Legal Process Outsourcing (LPO) industry after the global financial crisis, as the crisis led to an increase in cases of bankruptcy, auditory and regulatory compliances leading to litigations, mergers and acquisitions and cost pressures on firms. Subsequently, there was a surge in demand for documentation review and legal research work. The legal cells within the MNCs as well as other large firms decided to outsource this work on account of the rising expenses and shortage of in-house expertise.

India became a favoured destination for outsourced legal work, due to reasons such as the availability of a large pool of skilled English-speaking workforce, similarity of the Indian legal system with the US and the UK, IT services and domain-specific expertise of the Indian legal professionals at a much lesser cost. The Indian firms are expected to face competition from firms based in Vietnam, China, Hungary, the Czech Republic and the Philippines.

The Indian legal firms can tap developed markets such as the US and the UK, as well as the developing markets like France, Singapore, etc. Many of the countries in the African continent have developed their laws based on Indian statutes; hence, they are also important export destinations for LPO services from India.

The US houses 50 of the world's largest legal service provider firms, and has the highest number of legal service providers. India thus presents a unique opportunity as a market as well as a business base for extending their footprint and services to other nations. The Indian government is keen to liberalise the legal sector in a phased manner to attract more capital, create job opportunities and increase the export of legal services from India. It is in the process of taking few key reforms sought by the US firms as well by the Indian law firms. The pace of such reforms to be put into action post-approval needs to be increased.

The challenges faced by the Indian law firms need to be resolved with urgency:

- Law firms are prohibited from indulging in any form of advertising in India, which restricts them from building their brand. A brand provides more visibility and credibility to the firm, hence it is easier for them to market their domain expertise to their prospective clients. It is important to permit law firms to issue brochures, host websites, have directory listings, allow sponsorship of events etc., and other means of market development and information dissemination.
- Indian advocates are prohibited from charging a fee or have a profit-sharing agreement with any other entity. Further, advocates are restricted to increase their earning potential, as they cannot offer services such as accounting and tax management.
- The Indian lawyers are required to surrender their practice certificate to the State Bar Council, if they wish to enter into an employment contract with a foreign law firm.

The following suggestions can be considered for the growth of the LOP sector in India:

- The US and India must encourage law student exchange programmes between Indian and foreign universities, to aid students understand the profession, its requirements and the various challenges it faces.
- Industry-level seminars, workshops and training could be conducted by the government or the Bar Council of India (BCI) for imparting global standards and practices to Indian law professionals and imparting a better understanding of technology and knowledge management process, etc. The US-based lawyers are needed to conduct training for their Indian counterparts in order to enhance their service offerings.

- Work along with the American legal professionals to develop expertise in specific areas of law such as bankruptcy, intellectual property rights, patents, legal transcription, paralegal services and legal coding, corporate secretarial services, data entry, litigation support, reviewing and legal research etc., as per the demand pattern in the global market.
- The Indian government with BCI support can take initiative to help lawyers in raising capital from financial institutions for the establishment of larger firms with better infrastructure to support LPO. The government can also permit the US firms to invest, form joint ventures, collaborate or acquire Indian firms providing LPO services.
- Indian lawyers should be allowed to work with foreign firms, without the requirement of surrendering their practice certificate to the State Bar Council.
- Permit 100 per cent FDI for setting up legal firms, which would not only encourage employment growth but also an inflow of international business, greater knowledge transfer and ultimately the growth of the industry.
- Permit Multidisciplinary Practicing (MDP) firms employing lawyers, accountants, economists, taxation experts and management consultants, as it is required to provide a bouquet of advisory services. In this highly competitive sector, where specialisation is the order of the day, allowing MDP firms is critical if the Indian law firms have to compete with the leading firms in the world
- India imports many times of its exports in the legal services and the majority of that is for the reasons of arbitration, where India has a weakness. The UK, US and Singapore are few of the commercial arbitration hubs from where India imports legal services. It has the potential in itself to become an international arbitration and mediation services hub. The necessary architecture needs to be in place for the participation of foreign arbitrators in international commercial arbitration in India and India needs to develop an institutional framework for commercial arbitration as against the 'ad-hoc' arbitration prevalent in the country. Apart from

facilitating inexpensive and speedy justice for the domestic market, institutional arbitration can be a huge source of revenue for India. This can be achieved with the support and initiative of the government.

10. Summary

There are many other service exports sectors that are currently at a nascent stage and are still evolving. It is very important for the government to support and incubate them, as they may tomorrow be big game changers. It is no secret that India lacks infrastructural and capital support; it has the talent, but needs someone to back it up. That role can be fulfilled by the Americans. It is also in the US interest to support and help India; not only it provides it opportunity today to expand the American footprint in India but also provides it with the means and resources for furthering its interest in other developing markets. It provides the Americans security by a diversification of their markets, opportunity to introduce innovations, and have a ready work force for tomorrow.

India must focus on the following for a development of the service sectors in India as well as offering them to the world through exports:

A. Nurture India as a global innovation hub

- Strengthen intellectual property framework at par with global benchmarks
- Develop Centres of Excellence
- Embrace technology
- Provide world-class research infrastructure
- ICT solutions for healthcare, education, financial services, logistics, public services

B. Cultivating a high-calibre talent pool

- Improve quality of education and training
- Promote foreign language learning
- Scale up tertiary education and skill development
- Introduce reform in curriculum and faculty quality, stress on practical knowledge

- Provide exposure through student exchange programmes

C. Hub for technology entrepreneurship

- Incubation and mentorship
- Access to funding
- Capability development and capacity extension
- Market access

D. Establish India as a trusted hub for products

- Improve infrastructure
- Strengthen corporate governance
- Improve risk management and security
- Encourage global branding
- Robust and tested legal framework

E. Expand beyond core markets

- Reinvent business models
- Engage, Negotiate and Collaborate
- New verticals, geographies, customers
- Foster robust domestic demand
- Market extensively

END NOTES

1. https://www.ibef.org/economy/economic-survey-2015-16
2. https://www.ibef.org/economy/economic-survey-2015-16
3. The IT-BPM SECTOR IN INDIA: Strategic Review 2016, NASSCOM, 2016.
4. http://www.forbesindia.com/article/special/indian-itbpm-industry-clocks-growth-rate-of-8.6-percent-in-fy2017-nasscom/45951/1
5. http://www.forbesindia.com/article/special/indian-itbpm-industry-clocks-growth-rate-of-8.6-percent-in-fy2017-nasscom/45951/1
6. FICCI KPMG Background Paper for India Aviation, 2016
7. Airports Authority of India
8. Current Market Outlook 2015-2034, Boeing Forecast
9. http://www.oliverwyman.com/content/dam/oliver-wyman/v2/publications/2017/feb/2017%20Global%20Fleet%20MRO%20Market%20Forecast%20Summary%20Final_Short%20Version_1.pdf
10. http://www.oliverwyman.com/content/dam/oliver-wyman/v2/publications/2017/feb/2017%20Global%20Fleet%20MRO%20Market%20Forecast%20Summary%20Final_Short%20Version_1.pdf
11. http://www.prnewswire.com/news-releases/aviation-mro-market-in-india-2016-2020-300336879.html
12. https://www.ibef.org/industry/financial-services-india.aspx

13. http://www.amchamindia.com/PDF/KeyChallengesUS-%20IndiaEconomicEngagement.pdf
14. https://www.ibef.org/download/Engineering-design-and-development_20112.pdf
15. *"Travel & Tourism Economic Impact 2017 India". World Travel and Tourism Council.*
16. http://tourism.gov.in/sites/default/files/FTA/Press_Note_FTAs_Dec_16.PDF
17. http://edition.cnn.com/2016/01/19/travel/international-tourists-2015/
18. https://thepointsguy.com/2017/01/record-number-of-americans-traveled-abroad-2016/
19. http://www.business-standard.com/article/economy-policy/us-tourist-arrivals-to-india-on-the-rise-despite-advisories-117031100547_1.html
20. http://www.ndtv.com/india-news/indian-tourists-spent-over-13-billion-in-2016-in-america-us-embassy-1690127
21. http://medicaldialogues.in/771468-registered-practitioners-of-ayush-in-india-ministry/
22. Lunt, Neil, Richard Smith, Mark Exworthy, Stephen T. Green, Daniel Horsfall and Russell Mannion, 'Medical Tourism: Treatments, Markets and Health System Implications: A Scoping Review', Directorate for Employment, Labour and Social Affairs, p. 9. Accessed 03.29.16

SECTION 5

CONCLUSION

Winning the Presidential elections in the United States of America has been a definitive moment for Mr. Trump. It is a definitive moment for the US, and it casts its influence across the world. The issue is that despite being in office for around three months, the world still isn't sure about Trump and is in doubt about his policies and his approach.

Trump, till date, has maintained that he is guided by the principles of "America First", and "Hire American & Buy American". He has in one go moved far right from the policies being followed by the US. The US has been a strong supporter, motivator and campaigner of globalisation and the opening of world markets for trade. Trump has in one swoop has brushed this aside and at least in public, has taken a very protectionist, nationalistic stand and moved in the opposite direction of globalisation. This has confused the world as it still has not been able to judge whether there is a tectonic shift which is already occurring or is this a false bravado of Mr Trump. In both cases it has its impact on the world trade.

India is not left untouched with confused signals from the American President. The US is the largest market for Indian goods and service exports, and the protectionist stand undertaken by the American President is not in its interest. The contrary signals are also simultaneously being sent by the American administration that India is strategic to American plans and the relationship is going to be far much deeper and meaningful. There is no direct meeting that has taken place between the heads of the two nations. It gives India the necessary breather to gauge, re-calibrate and plan its approach towards Mr. Trump and his expectations from India.

The sense that comes out is that both the heads of nations have many common characteristics and both being quite independent in their decision-making and approach, being nationalists and yet practical in approach, it is going to be a favourable outcome. Trump takes pride in being a good dealmaker, and is focusing on bringing more business to the American shore; India has ample opportunities for him and the US business. Similarly, India is looking to expand its export base in the US and invite more FDI from the US businesses. Both of these objectives can be met provided that the economic agenda is delinked from the geopolitical agenda, which has been the bane of all the previous governments. Thankfully, Mr. Trump is not too much a follower of the traditional diplomatic route, and that provides an opportunity to the Indian Prime Minister to forge a direct relationship and take the economic agenda to the next level.

After scrapping TPP and issuing an executive order on a relook on NAFTA, the global community is wary of Trump. Trump would need to demonstrate his constructive achievements in the home country by forging new trade alliances, new bilateral treaties; he would be expecting a good deal from India. He would be expecting that India would present to him a proposition that would help him in his objectives. India needs to understand these expectations and it has the time to formulate such propositions. It has the opportunity to simultaneously look for solutions for its concerns. India will have to look beyond the H1B visas issue, as it is something which is going to undertake a course correction on its own, under the pressure from the American business houses themselves, when they realise that the Indian IT-BPM was providing them with the necessary edge and was arming the American businesses to fight out in the competitive global business. India must leverage its position and strength with Trump and must invite deeper investment ties and balance out the overreliance on China, Mexico and Canada. Trump has publically taken a position against China and later on retracted – this needs to be viewed with caution by India.

Summary

Trump is flexible and has an open-ended approach; he knows his job and will use his leverage. Trump is not a follower of tradition and has a mind of his own. He and his administration may seem too erratic or spontaneous, but there is a sure-shot deliberate calculative stance in it. The Indian government will have to be prepared and the following suggestions can be useful:

- Things will have to be kept simple, precise and short for Trump.
- The Indian Prime Minister must engage directly with Trump on common ground where both the parties agree upon and drive mileage, where both benefit. The approach would have to be personal, positive and pre-planned.
- The Indian policymakers should do their homework and must have multiple approaches or solutions, well thought of from the beginning for American issues.
- Focus on the people surrounding Trump to create a positive influence about India.
- Small capsules on how the Indian and American trade can be taken forward must be created and shared prior to his visit.
- The Indian government has to come up with a strategic plan that catches the imagination of Trump. The onus lies on India to take the relationship to the next level.
- An intent for defence, aviation and nuclear purchases from the United States can be helpful in grabbing Trump's attention.
- Robotics, energy and environment, advance engineering, transportation and logistics, healthcare are few other sectors where India is seeking help and investments should be promoted. These are not only high potential investment sectors but also where the American exports can benefit.
- The Indian government can engage with the Trump administration, through government-to-government procurement deals and lowering the trade barriers mutually.
- Resolve visa issues mutually for an easy access for businessmen and professionals; show flexibility on H1B visas.
- Apart from intensifying and expanding diplomatic relationship with the United States, other initiatives like trade meets and fairs should be organised on fast track to exchange and build on opportunities for both the nations.
- India must seek clarity and consistency in the new American President's policy towards China before it commits itself to any

trade deal with Trump, and must be wary of any American attempt to project India against China.

- Rather than being reactive, India should be proactively prepared. America needs access to the Indian market as much as we need access to theirs.
- Seek American investments into improving infrastructure and logistics.

India has to take a holistic overview of its approach to the exports as a whole, identify the gaps and plug them.

Suggestions and Recommendations

1. Market mapping in the US shall be taken up for a targeted and result-oriented policy push

a) ***State-wise:*** The 50 states of the US shall be scientifically mapped for Indian goods and service exports as the demand varies.

   i) **Hot spots:** where India ranks among the top 5 import partners of the US.

   ii) **Warm spots**: These could be the next 10 states where India is ranking among the top 15 import partners.

   iii) **Cold spots**: These would be the balance of states where India has a very stiff competition.

b) ***Sector-wise:*** Each of the 50 states needs to be mapped sector-wise to identify which are the sectors wherein imports are required.

   i) **Platinum sectors:** where India ranks among the top 5.

   ii) **Gold sectors**: these could be the next 10 sectors.

   iii) **Silver sectors**: the next top 10 sectors.

   The Indian trade bodies must concentrate on increasing their market share in the 'silver' sector; it needs to be aggressively pushed and supported by the Indian government through a policy framework and R&D support. The sectors in 'Platinum' and 'Gold' would need thorough assessments, and will need to be guarded as well as expanded to other states where there is a high potential for them. Sector mentors and product category experts must be engaged with the task to promote and bring awareness about Indian capabilities.

c) ***Product-wise:*** The top 25 products in each of the top 10 sectors for all states must be listed. Experts must be hired to undertake R&D in these top 25 product categories to help Indian manufacturers and exports develop products at par or far superior than those already in the American market.

2. Radical is the New Normal

The government must shift from the conventional way of working to adopting a radical approach by rejigging the existing organisational structure (currently 49 such bodies) looking after the Indian trade and exports. The Indian government must seriously consider creating an empowered apex body (like USTR) with professionals and top experts/talent hired or identified within the Indian Trade Service officers and Indian Foreign Service officers, operating on a day-to-day basis and which must guide and lead the trade negotiations and trade agenda.

3. Create a Robust Infrastructure, Logistics and Supply Chain Management

The growth of exports is linked directly to the growth of manufacturing and it is linked to infrastructure. Even in the service exports, the role of infrastructure cannot be ignored.

- **Power:** The availability of cheap power is the biggest challenge that India faces; this puts a big dent in manufacturing and production and even the service industry suffers due to a shortage of power. Experts estimate a 2-7 per cent loss in the entire life cycle of the product being exported, depending upon the electricity consumption for the production/storage of the finished goods. Hence, it requires urgent attention if the government is keen on increasing manufacturing and exports.
- **Logistics:** India is at the bottom in terms of its logistics infrastructure rating when compared to the major exporting nations in Asia. Transportation and logistics influence every stage of the export cycle. The priority of the Indian government should be to link the manufacturing hubs and the exports clusters to the ICD and ports. A new coastal road network, linking the ports, ICD and export-oriented townships/clusters, should be created for

an easy flow of goods, ranging from the movement of raw material to the dispatch of finished goods.

4. Laboratories and Auditing

The growth of Indian exports suffers due to large number of rejections. All such rejections could have been easily avoided if the exporters can be made aware of such issues in time. A concentrated attempt is required to bring Indian standards closer to international standards.

Labs not only help maintain quality, but also help in R&D, in introducing new processes, new technologies, new materials, innovations and in increasing productivity. They need to be an integral part of any infrastructure that the government plans in future for a manufacturing or exports cluster.

Labs also perform as an audit agency to monitor and suggest improvements; they point out deficiencies in the infrastructure, processes and environment, health and safety compliances.

5. Design Banks: Design as Differentiator

India ranks abysmally a mere 43 out of 45 countries in the global innovation index. The Indian companies are still focussing on the lower end of the value chain, especially for exports. They need to leap forward, and Research and Design can provide those wings.

India needs another movement like "Make in India" and "Digital India", to help create and establish Design Banks & Research Institutes (DBRI). The government can push various trade bodies and associations to create these design banks and research institutes. Like the CSR cess, the Indian companies shall willingly embrace the initiative and commit 1-2 per cent of their profits as their contribution for setting up these design banks. The Indian government can create an operating framework for the same and let the trade bodies, manufacturers and exporters benefit out of it.

6. Training, Training, Training...the Mantra for Success

The mantra to maintain timely quality deliverables is training – it helps being right every time. It helps inculcating an organisational culture and commitment towards quality, maintaining productivity and profitability. The adoption of TQM (Total Quality Management), TPM (Total Productivity Management), ISO (International Organisation for Standardisation), BS (British Standards), and JIT (Just in Time) would do a great good to Indian manufacturing and exports

Most of the current professional courses in exports are oriented towards marketing, trade documentation and custom clearances, and this too in metros. What India needs is all around training at every level of the trade process, and such training institutes shall be set up in all export clusters, with customised courses for each cluster requirement.

7. Financial Assistance

The government has been trying through various types of export schemes and incentives to attract manufacturers and service providers to exports. It has been rolling out doles to push exports. This approach has lived its life and is not going to be fruitful anymore. The existing approach of incentives to promote exports needs to be redefined and a course correction needs to be undertaken.

8. Grading

The central idea behind the existing categorisation is to provide incentives for the export target to be achieved. However, it does little in stating the quality of the exports or the deliverable timelines and client relationship. The same can be done easily by implementing and undertaking a new Grading & Certification of Indian Exporters, or by making relevant additions and modifications to protect the interest of international clients and to safeguard the Indian brands against adulterators, manipulators, thugs and repeat offenders. Each of the exporters must exhibit the grade while dealing with international clients. This will establish credibility amongst the world trading community. The government must link incentives and access to government facilities directly to the grading mechanism.

The grading mechanism shall be updated and reviewed every financial year and any change must reflect online as well as on the exporter's correspondence. The grading mechanism must also help the exporters have easy access to capital from financial institutes and other lenders.

9. Geographical Indication and Protection

Geographical Indication (GI) status is believed to be the oldest form of Intellectual Property (IP) protection. Supporters and campaigners of GI tags assert that GI is a differentiator and great marketing tool for the exporters, which can be used effectively 'to classify your produce and supplies at levels above your foreign competitors'. Some 258 GIs have been received and another 270 are in process, which in itself is proof enough of India's diversity, its rich traditional knowledge and craftsmanship, and if marketed properly can help artisans, craftsmen, farmers, weavers, etc., to further develop and produce to help Indian exports.

Presently, the GI awareness campaigns by the government appear to be concentrated only on the registration of GI products. It needs to come out with a strategic plan on promotion and branding.

Few recommendations that may be helpful are as follows:

a) Funding for promotion and marketing through corporate sponsorship by permitting them under the CSR initiative.
b) Establishing a network of watchdogs to report and protect infringement on the Indian GI.
c) Creating a consolidated data bank and design bank through scientific research and involving experts, who can help record the entire process and uniqueness in details.
d) The use of technology while labelling and branding. RFID tagging will help in detecting fakes.

10. Marketing and Promotions

One of the reasons for the earlier recommendation of "a radical approach" as required for the government is for jumpstarting the exports marketing and promotions in America and other countries.

Following are few of the recommendations:

a) Redesign Indian trade portals and websites of trade bodies etc. Digital marketing and Social media platforms shall be used to promote Indian products in American and other international markets.

b) Use of the outdoor medium for cost-efficient customised marketing to local requirements. Radio is another medium, which has the flexibility of size and customisation to target selected audience.
c) International celebrity endorsements as well engaging Indian celebrities to promote India and Indian goods.
d) Establishing a chain of experiential centres for encouraging locals to try out and experiment with Indian products, cuisines, handicrafts, consumer goods, etc. These centres can double up as market research as well as distribution points. The trade bodies can invest in these chains along with local investors keen to partner them.
e) Hold India-centric events, fairs, trade meets, etc., and engage with all stakeholders
f) Sponsor exchange programmes for training, education and research.
g) Create mega trade events in all parts of India to showcase and push exports.
h) International and national mentors and brand ambassadors shall be engaged and their services undertaken for promotions, as well as to provide insights, project trends and train Indian business houses.
i) Hire lobby groups and professional international exports promotion agencies to market and promote Indian products in new markets. This can be executed through trade bodies and councils.
j) Incentives for exposure to exporters, sponsoring workers, designers, engineers and technicians for international experience and participation in trade fairs, training meets and programmes for artisans and designers.

In the coming future, the Indian service sector and its exports is going to be the key driver of Indian growth. The US is not only India's biggest service import destination but can be a great enabler for India to achieve its goals. If the India–US trade relationship wishes to leap forward into the future, it will have to move the needle from "Dreaming to Doing".

The focus of the current government shall aim to give the Indian services the global visibility they rightly deserve. "Make in India" and "Digital India" initiatives are gaining momentum and are driving the expansion of the services in the domestic space in India as well as internationally.

However, a lot more needs to be done to unravel the true potential of the Indian services sector:

i) Lack of infrastructure is ailing the service exports as much as it affects the manufacturing and goods exports.
ii) A clear long-term vision for each of the key service sectors is required. Many services are under the purview of state governments or are jointly regulated by the central and state governments. The multiplicity of regulatory bodies creates multiplicity of regulations and multiple clearance requirements.
iii) The foundation of any policy framework is credible data and research. Lack of empirical research in the area of services export remains the biggest hurdle along with the lack of reliable, timely and easily interpretable data.
iv) Based on research and data available, the Government of India must formulate an Index of Services, in line with international practice, in order to have a coherent policy on services. Given the heterogeneity of services, a formulation of separate indices can also be considered.
v) Since the services sector is heterogeneous, it is important to identify the most important trade barriers faced by different services sub-sectors and then undertake sector-specific reforms.
vi) A blueprint to accomplish the goals for each service sector listed in the service index should be made.
vii) Accountability and responsibility alignment amongst stakeholders and a monitoring mechanism with reality checks need to be in place.
viii) The policy framework must stress upon the quality of services as well as their compliance to the international standards and laws.
ix) Majority of the services are exported from tier-2, tier-3 cities in different states; policies have to focus on state-wise requirements
x) A holistic and more practical view shall be aligned towards regulatory reforms and must follow international best practices.

xi) The same is essential to move away from the lower end of the value chain to the upper end.

The Indian companies can benefit from their early lead to set up knowledge and research hubs in the US and India to offer new innovative service solutions to the Americans. The Indo-US collaboration and partnership can boost innovation and new service categories as well as revolutionise the digital world and e-Commerce across the world. Artificial intelligence, 3D printing and robotics are going to transform the way humans live.

IT and digital services are influencing the way of governance, government-to-citizen (G2C), government-to-government (G2G), and government-to-business (G2B) interaction and other essential services like sanitation and municipal solid waste management services for the city. India can itself be a model for such service challenges and offer an opportunity to American as well as Indian companies to come up with solutions, which can help and be implemented in the "Indian Smart Cities" project to make them more habitable and connected. These digital solutions and services can be replicated for other developing nations.

Few of the opportunities in services where India and America can partner are Information Technology-Business Processing and Management (IT-BPM), government services and administration, space and satellite, aviation-maintenance repairs and overhaul, banking, insurance and other financial services, entertainment and soft media content development, engineering, architectural and other design services, tourism, hospitality and travel services, healthcare, wellness and medical tourism, accounting and auditing services, legal services, education and skills training, logistics, etc.

To conclude, the sense is that India and the US can mutually benefit if Trump and Modi are able to forge a personal connect and given the sensitivity, and trusting the acumen of both the nation heads, there is little possibility that they would let the opportunity slip away. So, we believe that the Indian foreign trade with the US will surely be trumped up.

ANNEXURES

ANNEXURE 1

India Rank in Imports in Various States in the United States of America

Indias rank in imports by states in the United States of America										
State name	Rank	val2013	val2014	val2015	val2016	share13	share14	share15	share16	change
Alabama	19	91.67	115.49	140.63	149.84	0.484	0.5192	0.6426	0.6759	6.55
Alaska	18	3.64	4.75	2.15	5.27	0.2456	0.2355	0.0863	0.2526	145.03
Arizona	14	175.58	193.61	224.4	213.94	0.923	0.9806	1.1364	1.0883	-4.66
Arkansas	6	208.66	209.38	236.72	183.12	2.7379	2.7516	2.9923	2.3385	-22.64
California	17	3365.11	4395.87	3856.38	3634.02	0.8831	1.0886	0.9446	0.8856	-5.77
Colorado	12	376.42	311.46	214.31	210.81	2.936	2.1841	1.5865	1.7237	-1.63
Connecticut	17	194.48	284.01	271.36	245.28	0.9019	1.1874	1.045	1.1494	-9.61
District of Colombia	1	33.51	236.74	140.17	80.74	5.3553	21.4247	15.3543	16.5507	-42.4
Florida	15	891.51	1219.94	1143.99	1401.18	1.2338	1.6979	1.5583	1.9009	22.48
Georgia	8	1608.23	1846.69	2103.44	2123.77	2.1436	2.2016	2.3724	2.4634	0.97
Illinois	16	1192.53	1367.49	1416.08	1425.34	0.9558	0.9743	1.1676	1.1726	0.65
Indiana	19	393.05	428.38	405.35	384.81	0.8605	0.876	0.826	0.7761	-5.07
Iowa	7	133.98	151.49	165.82	204.89	1.4	1.5017	1.771	2.4849	23.56
Kansas	19	69.15	95.6	82.71	99.28	0.6428	0.8095	0.7026	0.8896	20.04
Kentucky	8	859.09	845.79	1176.64	1913.19	2.2691	2.1493	3.0436	4.7817	62.6
Massachusetts	22	279.41	303.79	298.31	309.95	0.8132	0.8799	0.8865	0.9158	3.9
Maryland	17	415.76	712.45	537.25	430.4	1.5643	2.3673	1.7046	1.4042	-19.89
Maine	22	25.44	30.51	19.47	19.65	0.7185	0.7891	0.5283	0.5871	0.94
Michigan	8	1131.58	998.66	935.32	1010.11	0.9577	0.8121	0.7529	0.7483	8
Minnesota	14	195.78	197.84	215.87	218.72	0.5929	0.5694	0.7552	0.8095	1.32
Missouri	9	351.18	439.34	395.1	348.15	1.8968	2.3948	2.1344	2.0204	-11.88
Mississippi	15	295.99	193.67	213.46	176.09	1.4797	1.1204	1.5156	1.2597	-17.51
Montana	18	9.14	66.54	21.65	2.28	0.1593	1.0667	0.5327	0.0652	-89.46
North Carolina	10	1176.12	1300.85	1345.58	1249.49	2.3594	2.458	2.6246	2.6526	-7.14
North Dakota	6	53.62	59.14	73.82	75.88	1.4889	1.5447	2.3526	2.9578	2.79
Nebraska	10	32.42	24.94	50.59	70.98	0.8754	0.6152	1.2232	1.9939	40.32
New Hampshire	7	127.44	141.9	161.66	151.86	1.0733	1.2634	1.7359	1.7636	-6.06
New Jersey	3	5704.61	6428.93	6290.3	6139.82	4.7837	5.0835	5.2586	5.6713	-2.39
New Mexico	9	18.23	17.86	16.33	28.03	0.9042	0.8001	0.7261	1.2237	71.65
Nevada	7	114.98	169.47	221.4	262.8	1.3397	2.1568	2.3075	2.4875	18.7
New York	3	10456.48	10555.83	10615.29	11851.31	8.059	7.838	7.9725	9.1038	11.64
Ohio	9	1011.37	1346.86	1398.63	1431.05	1.5227	1.9135	2.0294	2.2246	2.32
Oklahoma	12	165.81	214.77	209.5	110.14	1.3391	1.5763	1.902	1.2961	-47.43
Oregon	17	119.36	189.84	140.68	132.34	0.8321	1.376	0.9491	0.7515	-5.93
Pennsylvania	11	1093.12	1176.25	1445.54	1961.26	1.2869	1.4137	1.8127	2.5407	35.68
Puerto Rico	19	180.46	245.67	211.29	261.92	0.7468	1.0486	1.0794	1.2335	23.96
Rhode Island	17	117.7	55.05	52.41	51.3	1.2301	0.6587	0.6363	0.5863	-2.12
South Carolina	8	719.41	834.96	922.01	840.26	2.1867	2.2086	2.3618	2.3254	-8.87
South Dakota	14	4.81	6.33	7.02	6.34	0.4816	0.6074	0.6155	0.6146	-9.65
Tennessee	10	1306.63	984.08	1429.62	1599.99	2.0107	1.4097	1.8571	2.1232	11.92
Texas	17	4288.54	4050.72	3330.94	2388.06	1.3758	1.3375	1.321	1.0414	-28.31
Utah	18	65.05	116.64	85.11	98.6	0.6115	1.0478	0.7033	0.7586	15.85
Virginia	9	798.43	728.8	754.23	794.47	3.5671	2.997	3.0093	3.0686	5.34
Virgin Islands	3	5.7	30.93	3.04	44.51	1.2348	4.5002	2.3201	9.0218	1365.92
Vermont	6	69.16	68.92	64.99	59.27	1.3974	1.4465	1.5996	1.5895	-8.81
Washington	18	341.85	386.81	452.73	362.63	0.6851	0.7362	0.8857	0.7674	-19.9
Wisconsin	8	639.01	677.82	674.22	636.45	2.8754	2.8766	2.9256	2.8352	-5.6
West Virginia	8	126.86	65.97	64.36	52.58	3.4274	1.7303	1.7018	1.5773	-18.3
Wyoming	13	21.97	7.33	6.96	3.39	1.0163	0.3858	0.6079	0.3863	-51.33

Source: https://www.census.gov/foreign-trade/statistics/state/index.html

ANNEXURE 2

List of Attached, Subordinate Offices, Autonomous Bodies, Public Sector Undertakings, Export Promotion Councils and Other Organisations under the Department of Commerce*

Attached Offices

1. Directorate General of Foreign Trade, Udyog Bhavan, New Delhi – 110107.
2. Directorate General of Supplies & Disposals, Jeevan Tara Building, Parliament Street, New Delhi - 110001.
3. Directorate General of Anti-Dumping & Allied Duties, Jeevan Tara Building, 4th Floor, 5, Parliament Street, New Delhi-110001. Ph.: 011-23348653, 23348654

Subordinate Offices

1. Directorate General of Commercial Intelligence and Statistics, 565, Anandapur, Ward No. 108, Sector– 1, Plot No. 22, ECADP Kolkata – 700107
2. Cochin Special Economic Zone, Administrative Building, Kakkanad, Kochi, Kerala.
3. Falta Special Economic Zone, IInd MSO Building, 4th Floor, R.No. 44, Nizam Palace Complex, 234/4, AIC Bose Road, Kolkata – 700020, West Bengal.
4. MEPZ Special Economic Zone, National Highway 45, Administrative Office Building, Tambaram, Chennai – 600045, Tamil Nadu.

---

*http://commerce.gov.in/writereaddata/uploadedfile/MOC_636281140249481285_annual_report_16_17_eng.pdf

5. Kandla Special Economic Zone, Gandhidham, Kutch-370230, Gujarat.
6. SEEPZ Special Economic Zone, Andheri (East), Mumbai – 400096, Maharashtra.
7. Visakhapatnam Special Economic Zone, Administrative Building, Duvvada, Visakhapatnam – 530046, Andhra Pradesh.
8. Noida Special Economic Zone, Noida Dabri Road, Phase-II, Noida – 201305, Distt. Gautam Budh Nagar, Uttar Pradesh.
9. Pay and Accounts Office (Commerce), Udyog Bhavan, New Delhi - 110107.
10. Pay and Accounts Office (Supply Division), 16-A, Akbar Road Hutments, New Delhi

Autonomous Bodies

1. Coffee Board, 1, Dr. B.R. Ambedkar Veedhi, Bangalore – 560001, Karnataka.
2. Rubber Board, Sub-Jail Road, P.B. No.1122, Kottayam – 686002, Kerala.
3. Tea Board, 14, BTM Sarani, Brabourne Road, P.B. No.2172, Kolkata – 700001, West Bengal.
4. Tobacco Board, P.B. No.322, Guntur – 522004, Andhra Pradesh.
5. Spices Board, Sugandha Bhavan, N.H. Bypass, PB-2277, Palarivattom P.O. Kochi – 682025, Kerala.
6. Marine Products Export Development Authority, MPEDA House, Panampilly Avenue, Kochi – 682036, Kerala. 7. Agricultural & Processed Food Products Export Development Authority, NCUI Building, Siri Institutional Area, August Kranti Marg, New Delhi – 110016.
7. Export Inspection Council of India, 3rd Floor, NDYMCA Cultural Centre Building, 1, Jai Singh Road, New DelhI-110001.
8. Indian Institute of Foreign Trade, B-21, Institutional Area, South of IIT, New Delhi – 110016.
9. Indian Institute of Packaging, B-2, MIDC Area, P.B. No. 9432, Andheri (East), Mumbai – 400096,

Public Sector Undertakings

1. State Trading Corporation of India, Jawahar Vyapar Bhavan, Tolstoy Marg, New Delhi - 110001.
2. STCL Ltd., No. 7A, "STC Trade Centre", 3rd Floor, Nandini Layout, Bengaluru – 560096, Karnataka.
3. MMTC Ltd., Scope Complex, 7, Institutional Area, Lodhi Road, New Delhi - 110003.
4. PEC Ltd.,"Hansalaya", 15, Barakhamba Road, New Delhi - 110001.
5. Export Credit Guarantee Corporation of India Ltd., 10th Floor, Express Towers, P.B. No. 373, Nariman Point, Mumbai - 400021, Maharashtra.
6. India Trade Promotion Organization, Pragati Maidan, Mathura Road, New Delhi – 110001.

Export Promotion Councils

1. Chemexcil, Jhansi Castle (4th Floor), 7 Cooperage Road, Mumbai-400039.
2. Cashew EPC, P.B. No.1709, Chittoor Road, Ernakulam South, Cochin-682016
3. CAPEXIL, Vanijya Bhavan, International Trade Facilitation Centre, 1/1 Wood Street, 3rd Floor, Kolkata-700016.
4. Council for Leather Exports, No.1, CMDA Tower II, 3rd Floor, Gandhi Irwin Road, Egmore, Chennai-600008.
5. EEPC India, Vanijya Bhavan, International Trade Facilitation Centre, 1st Floor, 1/1 Wood Street, Kolkata-700016
6. Export Promotion Council for EOUs & SEZ Units, 8-G, Hansalaya, 15, Barakhamba Road, New Delhi-110001.
7. Gem & Jewellery EPC, Diamond Plaza, 5th Floor, 391-A, Dr. D.B. Marg, Mumbai- 400004.
8. The Plastic EPC, Crystal Tower, Gundivali Road No.3, Off Sir M.V. Road, Andheri East, Mumbai- 400069.
9. Sports Goods EPC, 1-E/6, Swami Ram Tirth Nagar, Jhandewalan Extn., New Delhi- 110055.
10. Shellac Export Promotion Council, Vanijya Bhavan, International Trade Facilitation Centre, 2nd Floor, 1/1 Wood Street, Kolkata-700016.

11. Pharmexcil, 101, Aditya Trade Centre, Ameerpet, Hyderabad, Andhra Pradesh – 500038.
12. Services EPC, 509, 5th Floor, Apparel House, Sector 44, Institutional Area, Gurgaon-122003.
13. Project EPC, 123, I Floor, Behind Shankar Road Market, New Rajinder Nagar, New Delhi – 110060
14. Indian Oilseeds and Produce Exporters Association, 78-79 Bajaj Bhawan, Nariman Point, Mumbai-400021.

Other Organisations

1. Federation of Indian Export Organizations, Niryat Bhawan, Rao Tula Ram Marg, Opp. Army Hospital (Research& Referral), New Delhi-110057.
2. Indian Diamond Institute, Katargam, GIDC, Sumul Dairy Road, P.B. No. 508, Surat-395008, Gujarat.
3. Footwear Design & Development Institute, A-10/A, Sector-24, Noida – 201301, Gautam Budh Nagar, Uttar Pradesh.
4. National Centre for Trade Information, NCTI Complex, Pragati Maidan, New Delhi - 110001.
5. Price Stabilisation Fund Trust, Room No.2003. 20th Floor, Jawahar Vyapar Bhawan, Tolstoy Marg, Connaught Place. New Delhi - 110001

ANNEXURE 3

India's Trade in 2015–16

India's merchandise exports reached a level of US$ 262.00 billion during 2015–16(P) registering a negative growth of 15.57 per cent as compared to a negative growth of 1.29 per cent during the previous year. Despite the recent setback faced by India's export sector due to the global slowdown, merchandise exports recorded a compound annual growth rate (CAGR) of 8.43 per cent from 2006–07 to 2015–16 (P). During the year 2015–16 (P), the cumulative value of exports was US$ 262.00 billion as against US$ 310.34 billion over the corresponding period of the previous year registering a negative growth of 15.57 per cent. Cumulative value of imports for the year 2015–16 (P) was US$ 380.36 billion as against US$ 448.03 billion during the corresponding period of the previous year registering a negative growth of 15.11 per cent. The trade deficit in April–March 2015-16 (P) was estimated at US$ 118.35 billion which was lower than the deficit of US$ 137.70 billion during 2014–15.*

India's share in the world merchandise exports remained stagnant at 1.6 per cent in 2015 from a level of 1.69 per cent in 2014 mainly on account of a modest and uneven recovery in advanced economies. Similarly, India's share in world commercial services exports has slightly increased from 3.15 per cent in 2014 to 3.3 per cent in 2015.**

* http://commerce.gov.in/writereaddata/uploadedfile/MOC_636281140249481285_annual_report_16_17_eng.pdf

**http://commerce.gov.in/writereaddata/uploadedfile/MOC_636281140249481285_annual_report_16_17_eng.pdf

INDEX